MIRACLES OF LOVE

ACKNOWLEDGEMENTS

I dedicate this book to my devoted wife, Betty, acknowledging her prayers and support during my many years of traveling while she remained at home to keep everything in order.

This book was written because of my Lord Jesus Christ's Power to transform lives, such as my own. I pray that this book will encourage believers to come closer to God, and unbelievers to join the Family of God.

All incidents in this book are true, and God involved the author in each one. However, the author has sought to protect the identity of those referred to in this book, except where permission has been given. Otherwise, names have been changed.

I praise God for each one of you whom my Lord has given me as a friend and brother in Christ. Each one of you has greatly enriched my life.

MIRACLES
OF LOVE

by Coach Floyd Eby

DISTRIBUTORS
A Division of Baker Book House
Grand Rapids, Michigan 49506

MIRACLES OF LOVE

ISBN: 0-8010-3384-5

First printing, November 1978
Second printing, June 1979
Third printing, June 1980
Fourth printing, August 1981
Fifth printing, June 1982
Sixth printing, June 1984

OTHER BOOKS BY THE AUTHOR
CALLING GOD'S TOWER...COME IN, PLEASE!
CHAMPIONS FOREVER

MIRACLES OF LOVE
Copyright 1978 by Floyd Eby, Coldwater, Michigan

Printed in the United States of America

INTRODUCTION

This is a book about God's power. I have seen how His power has worked to transform many lives; how it has changed so many people, bringing happiness, peace of mind, and a new way of life to them. I was fortunate to be the instrument of God's love, to be used by Him, to present this wonderful way of life to many people who needed Jesus in their lives. I was merely the instrument. God had already prepared them, before I came along.

But I would like to take you along with me, in this book, to see how the transformation worked for others so that you can see how it might work for you.

God opened many doors for me, in churches, schools, jails, hospitals, sanitariums, mental institutions, homes, communes, courts, clinics, hotels, motels; to hitchhikers, flyers, businessmen, neighbors, friends, relatives, most often to complete strangers. And wherever and whenever God opened the door, I have tried to enter. Come with me on some of these experiences.

I pray that this book will be used through God's will to bring unbelievers into the Family of God, to stimulate believers to be more active in spreading the Good News about our wonderful Saviour, to help believers get closer to God with even more assurance of His Wonderful love, compassion and power.

I have covenated with the Lord that all monies derived from the sale of this book will be used entirely in the missionary work of our Lord Jesus Christ. God has already taken care of my daily needs.

If God in some way uses this book to help you to become a believer, or to become strengthened in the faith, or to become active in carrying His message to others, won't you please write to me or call me so that I may put you on my prayer list? If you will send your photograph I will put it on my prayer board. And I will also try to visit you as the Lord opens the door and makes time available. There is absolutely no cost or obligation to you.

May our Lord bless you.

Floyd Eby
15 Cardinal Drive
Coldwater, Michigan 49036

(517) 278-5031

CONTENTS

Acknowledgements

Introduction

About The Author

Preface

Chapter 1	*God Is My Pilot*	19
Chapter 2	*Time Is Running Out*	36
Chapter 3	*Our Future Life Guaranteed*	51
Chapter 4	*Turning Problems Into Joy*	66
Chapter 5	*Christianity Doesn't Always Work*	84
Chapter 6	*Ministry Of Love*	102
Chapter 7	*Spreading The Good News*	120
Chapter 8	*Miracles From God*	134
Chapter 9	*Praise The Lord*	151
Chapter 10	*Things Are Different Now*	165

ABOUT THE AUTHOR

Coach Eby pictured below as he appears now in serving His Lord Jesus full time as speaker, evangelist, missionary, lay witness, counselor, and Gideon distributing the Word of God. Coach Eby also holds Bible studies in homes. Coach Floyd Eby has a wife, Betty, two daughters and four grandchildren.

Coach Floyd Eby has been credited by many coaches and fans as the orginator of the basketball full court zone press, "race horse" basketball, and the one handed jump shot as early as 1939. Coach Eby was also the originator of the football open huddle, defensive huddle and the split T offense. God has guided Coach Eby into many endeavors:
1.) Master of Science degree plus ten credits toward a Doctorate from Michigan State University at East Lansing, Michigan.
2.) Taught Science 30 years in the secondary public schools

of Michigan. Selected Teacher of the Year in the State of Michigan in 1965.

3.) Coached 25 years as head coach in basketball, and other sports such as football, baseball, and track for a lesser number of years. The coaching career included many championships, including two State Championships in basketball, but even more important included so many opportunities to witness for his Saviour to so many young people.

4.) State President of the Michigan Gideons for three years.

5.) Two years overseas in the United States Navy during World War Two as Communications Officer on a Destroyer Escort.

6.) He flies his own plane approximately 60,000 miles per year, and the Lord has given him the opportunity to give over 200 messages each year including athletic banquets, church banquets, Junior and Senior high schools, college groups, pulpit supply and Gideon messages throughout the midwest.

7.) He has also been engaged in many business enterprises: Cablevision, Building Contracting Business, Modular Homes, Mobile Homes, Financing, Sub-division, Insurance, Real Estate, Sports Announcer, and Frozen Foods. The above made it possible for him to serve his Lord, and pay his own way with funds supplied by his Lord through the above enterprises.

8.) He has also had the opportunity to work with over 3000 people in the Midwest and other states: telling about God's wonderful plan for their lives, seeing them join the Family of God, and then follow-up with them with visits, letters and phone calls, as well as home Bible studies to encourage them to grow spiritually. He has over 3000 people on his prayer list.

9.) Selected for State High School Coaches Hall of Fame in 1964.

10.) Elected Outstanding Citizen of Coldwater, Michigan, his home town, in 1976 by the Greater Coldwater Area Chamber of Commerce.

11.) Author of books, *"Calling God's Tower, Come In Please,* and *"Champions Forever."*

MIRACLES OF LOVE

PREFACE

The twenty year old girl on the front cover is Melanie
Hagemyer. Melanie received Jesus as a young child. After
graduating from high school, she attended a Christian
College. After two years of college, Melanie fell out of
fellowship with her Lord.

Due to some mistakes in her spiritual life, Melanie was
overloaded with a guilt complex. She felt she had lost her
salvation, and that she was going to hell. She felt she
couldn't live this way and wanted to get it over with.

While Melanie was home, she attempted to hang herself.
Fortunately, her father found her in time, and untied her

before she suffocated. Her parents entered her in a Christian mental hospital for treatment. As Melanie stated, "the hospital kept me from taking my life, but it did not have any answers for me."

Sometime after Melanie had been discharged from the mental hospital, she once again came face to face with Jesus. As Melanie likes to put it, "I was healed."

Melanie is now taking an active part in the ministry of "Calling God's Tower Ministries." She is participating as a singer, counselor, and telling others about Jesus as a personal witness. Melanie will not offend people, but if they are willing, she will tell anyone about this wonderful new way of life!

Following Is Melanie's Story and Testimony
My Dark Shadow

During February of 1977, a change took place in my life. The months that followed held the darkest, most miserable days of my life.

I was an average high school student. My social life was good although I did little dating. I participated in such activities as cheerleading, basketball, gymnastics, and future homemakers.

I seemingly knew what I wanted out of life. I wanted to find the will of God for my life and to do His Will. At the age of seven, I became what is known as a born-again Christian. At the age of twelve I gave my whole life to God.

From then on I became known in school as Miss Churchy, The Reverend Mother, and Sister Hagemyer. Knowing I had someone worth living for and talking about, I cared little what names people called me. I loved Jesus and I couldn't understand why so many others didn't.

After graduating in 1975, I attended Grand Rapids School of the Bible and Music the following fall. What else would you expect such a spiritual creature as myself to do?

The following summer I went to Montana as a summer missionary. Upon returning to school, I met a special guy whom I dated on a regular basis for the next eight months. Soon after Christmas we decided to break up. About a month later some problems that I know now were building up inside me for a long time began to surface. I had taken a heavy study load that semester which made me over tired and that didn't help the situation at all.

It was as if a dark shadow had come into my life and was following me wherever I went. I lost self-confidence. It became almost impossible for me to rise in the morning. My schedule said yes, but my mind and body said no. I found it very difficult to look anyone in the eyes, especially my fellow students. I didn't understand what was happening to me. I began to doubt the validity of my faith.

Soon after this, thoughts of suicide came. I was horrified! I had never had such thoughts before, and now I couldn't control them. Each time I passed a window I saw myself jumping out.

As the days passed, my thought patterns became jumbled, and I couldn't think or react normally. I became very depressed and physically worn out. Soon the smile, that in times past, had been warm and bright upon my face, disappeared. My eyes, usually full of life, simply died. Friends noticed the difference. They tried to help me, but their efforts were of no effect. My last three weeks of school were sheer hell for me.

Upon returning home, my state of mind became worse. My activities each day would consist of eating, sleeping, pacing, and reading romantic books. I was now convinced that I had lost my salvation and was on my way to hell.

No one who knew the old Melanie could believe this new person I had suddenly become. I quickly gained weight due to overeating and sleeping so much. I let my appearance go.

Not long after returning home from school, I decided to go to Cincinnati, Ohio, to work in the inner city as a summer missionary. Due to my emotional state, I failed miserably and returned home after only five weeks.

After being home for a short while, I attempted suicide. I failed due to my father saving me before it was too late. Being almost frantic by this time, my parents decided to take me to a psychiatrist. After one visit the therapist recommended that I be hospitalized. I was signed into Pine Rest Christian Hospital in Grand Rapids, Michigan.

As I begged mom not to leave me there, one of the patients walked up to me and grabbed my hand. He proceeded to tell me what a nice place it was, and how much I was going to like it. Being half hysterical, I snatched my hand away, and hugged my mom. I couldn't help thinking of how terrible this place was going to be.

Have you ever smelled hospital sheets? Have you ever slept with a bottle of bleach? It was all I could do not to find a way to break through to the out of doors and grasp some fresh air. I'm from a farm and to me cow manure would have been more welcome to my nostrils than those sheets.

My first roommate was of no help. She talked and swore a lot; usually with, and at, people who were not there. She kept saying that she hated people. I thought, "now wait a minute, I am a person. If anyone is going to kill me, it is going to be me."

Upon being there a few weeks, I began to understand her. I felt pity for her. Her mind was damaged due to the use of drugs. One day after I had been moved to a different room, she came in, sat down, and looked me straight in the eyes. She said, "I like you, I really like you. Will you be my friend?"

I felt terrible because I knew I couldn't help her although I did agree to be her friend. I knew she was worse off than I. Yet I couldn't see hope so I continued to wallow in my self-pity.

I was hospitalized for eight weeks. During this time I experienced a variety of things. I met a number of different people, and for the most part I remained in one state of mind --- depressed --- while I was there. After eight weeks of trying to help me, the doctors gave up.

I didn't want to follow any of the therapy, so that left their hands tied. They wanted to discharge me, only if I made some definite plans for my future. I couldn't do that. At one thousand dollars per week, I had to do something. I signed out, against medical advice, convinced that I would be dead within two weeks after returning home.

Apart from weighing twenty pounds more, having pimples, and getting my hair cut, I was the same when I arrived home as when I left. My state of depression lasted three more months during which time my daily life was still mostly eating and sleeping.

I had many sleepless nights. My dreams were often weird and frightening. One I distinctly remember took place while I was in Cincinnati. The scene was my mother's church nursery. I was in the nursery with a science teacher from high school. We were talking when suddenly an intruder entered and proceeded to attack me.

It was a thirty pound rat. As it moved toward me, I drew my arm back and thrust my fist into its stomach. I could feel my hand penetrating the rat's stomach. At this point I was thoroughly grossed out and frightened.

I woke up and began to cry. My immediate thought was, "Will this ever end? Is this what hell will be like? I don't want to go there! Please God, I don't want to go there!"

During the months that followed my hospitalization, my parents simply let me alone to do my own thing. Mom kept trying to get me to do things and go to church, but I just wouldn't. So there I was, a human being, living as a vegetable, drowning in depression and self-pity. Each day left only the thought that tomorrow would be my last day.

Finally after three months of this, I was fed up with the whole situation. I knew I needed God again, and I desperately wanted Him. I no longer wished to die although I knew I would if I didn't start to fight. I wanted to believe that I was a Christian. I wanted forgiveness for all the wrong in my life during those months of despair.

I had hated God and I had told Him so. I deserved nothing but hell and death and I knew it.

One night in February, directly after a long telephone conversation with a friend, I went into my Mom's bedroom and got down on my knees. I began to pray:

"Dear God, I need you so badly! I know you died for me, and I believe you still love me although I know I don't deserve it. If you are not in my heart already, I receive you now. I choose to repent of my sin. Dear Jesus, take my life from this moment forward and glorify yourself in me. Please show me scripture to give me assurance God, and thank you, Lord. Thank you so much! I love you! In Jesus name I pray, Amen."

Directly after I prayed, Satan came to me with the same old story. "You don't mean it. You're not saved and you never will be. Look what you have done!"

This time I was ready to fight and I let him have it with both barrels. I said something to this effect, "Look Satan, Jesus said if I turned from my sin and gave my heart to Him, He would save me. He is God and He doesn't lie. You are the chief of liars, Satan. I regret very much listening to your lies for all these months. I now choose to believe God! So you can just pack up your lies and go straight to hell where you belong!"

From then on I began reading my Bible again every morning. The Lord answered my prayer concerning assurance and He gave me Psalm Three to claim as my own.

"Lord, how are they increased that trouble me! Many are they that rise up against me. Many there be which say of my Soul, There is no help for him in God. But thou, O Lord, art a shield for me; my Glory, and the lifter up of my head. I cried unto the Lord with my voice, and He heard me out of His holy hill. I laid me down and slept; I awaked; for the Lord sustained me. I will not be afraid of ten thousands of people, that have set themselves against me round about. Arise, O Lord; save me, O my God: for thou hast smitten all mine enemies upon the cheek bone; thou hast broken the teeth of the ungodly. Salvation belongeth unto the Lord: thy blessing is upon thy people.

Since I repented, the Lord has given me new life and hope. I love Him so much more now that I ever did before. I plan on finishing my Christian Education in the fall.

My goals for the future include working with orphans and prisoners, directing a childrens' choir, learning to play the guitar well, singing praises unto Jesus, making a record, and writing a book. I even hope to eventually marry and raise a family. I desire the perfect will of God and I know He will give it to me. *Proverbs 3:5-6 "Trust in the Lord with all thine heart, and lean not unto thine own understanding. In all thy ways acknowledge Him, and He shall direct thy paths."*

After all that has happened to me, I wonder how so many people survive without trusting Him. Looking at the suicide rate shows me that many of them don't.

It is my hope and prayer that my story and testimony will be of encouragement to all of you. May God draw you close to Himself, for in His presence is fullness of joy! May He richly bless your life as He has mine.

Yes, this time in my life was a dark shadow, almost like a tunnel with no end. But, praise God, at the end of the tunnel was *The Light*, just waiting for me with open arms!

"Jesus saith unto him, I am the way, the truth, and the Life; no man cometh unto the Father, but by me."
John 14:6

Melanie Hagemyer

*"Who are these that fly like a cloud,
and like the doves to their windows?"*
Isaiah 60:8

1

GOD IS MY PILOT

On a late afternoon in September, I was flying my skyhawk plane out of Murphy, North Carolina, headed toward Ashland, Kentucky. Andrews Field at Murphy was surrounded by mountains six or seven thousand feet high. After taking off I circled my plane around and around the field until I had reached the safe altitude.

I flew over the mountains underneath the clouds, and I was having difficulty with visibility because of haze. I looked up and saw many large holes in the clouds above me. I radioed a weather station and I was assured that the cloud ceiling was going to remain broken on my entire trip to Ashland.

I immediately pulled back on my wheel, and scooted up through one of the numerous holes.

Up on top it was beautiful. The sun was shining and the visibility was unlimited. This was really great, I thought. I could see the mountains, small towns, and houses below me through the holes in the clouds and through the haze below the clouds.

After about eighty miles, the holes in the clouds started disappearing.

Basic flying rules called for a VFR pilot, which is my rating, to reverse 180 degrees and go back and find a hole and then go below and stay underneath the clouds.

I spotted a hole over to my right several miles, and decided that would save me the mileage and time of going back. I "guesstimated" that by now I was out of the mountains, although I had been unable to see the ground terrain for some time.

After I reached the hole to my right which was quite small, I started circling down through it. Sometimes I would lose the hole and find myself in solid clouds. I then tried to locate the hole once again. When I did, I looked up and could see mountains all around me. The tops were buried in white, snowy, billowy clouds.

Immediately I knew I was trapped in the mountains, and in a desperate situation.

As I kept circling downward, I grabbed for my mike.

"Lexington approach, this is Cessna 5750 Romeo, come in please."

"Cessna 5750 Romeo, this is Lexington approach."

Praise God I could still reach them even though I was below the mountain tops, and a long distance from Lexington.

"Lexington approach, this is 50 Romeo, I am trapped in the mountains somewhere in North Carolina. I am squawking 1200 on my transponder. Please contact me on radar."

I was now praying that I was still high enough for them to pick me up on radar.

"50 Romeo, Lexington approach. Squawk 4235."

"50 Romeo to approach, I am squawking 4235 and ident."

"50 Romeo, we have picked you up on radar. Are you instrument rated?"

"Negative," I answered.

I was trying to stay on instruments. Every time I lost the hole and got into solid clouds, I knew I had to find the hole but quick or crash into the side of the mountain. I preferred the hole.

"50 Romeo. Lexington approach. Can you handle instruments?"

I was in a very critical situation trying to keep my plane in the hole, fly instruments, check my chart, and talk on the radio. Approach was still asking me routine questions. At least they seemed routine to me -- because I expected to crash into a mountain any second.

"Approach, this is 50 Romeo, and I need help now," I shouted as loud as I could into the mike.

"50 Romeo. Approach. If you are sure you can handle instruments, we will send you up through the clouds, because there is no traffic in that area at the present."

"Let's get going," I urged. I pulled back on my wheel and started up through the soup.

"What are the tops of the mountains in this area?" I asked.

"7000 feet," was the answer.

I now felt safer as I plowed through the clouds, watching my instruments to keep level and in a stable climb. My altimeter now read 7500 feet.

"Lexington approach, this is 50 Romeo. What are you going to do with me after you get me up on top?"

"We will talk about that after you get there," was the answer. "You will break out at 8500 feet."

At 8500 feet I still couldn't see a thing. At 9500 feet, I was still in the soup. At 10,500, visibility was still zero. I was still flying blind at 11,000 feet.

I realized that my situation was now desperate again, because my skyhawk, under the most ideal conditions, will only fly 12,000 feet high. If I didn't break out before I reached my plane's ceiling, I would have to come down through the soup on instruments. Most certainly I would hit the top of a mountain.

Praise God, I broke out on top and into the sunshine at 11,400 feet. I grabbed the mike and yelled, "Lexington approach, this is 50 Romeo, I broke out on top at 11,400 feet."

"50 Romeo, Lexington approach. A pilot reported a hole 30 miles northeast of your position. Steer 032 and we will bring you down through that hole. You will then be out of the mountains."

I steered 032 for 15 minutes, but in no way could I find that reported hole in the clouds, and I reported this to Lexington. They sent me a different direction for another reported hole, but still no success.

"Lexington approach. 50 Romeo. I only have 90 minutes of fuel left. I have to be going to some definite place to set down. I am heading toward Lexington."

"50 Romeo, there is no use coming this far. We only have two holes in our area and they will be gone before you get here."

"I don't care," I answered. "I have to come some place and I have decided it will be Lexington."

They accepted my decision, and started talking to me about coming down through the clouds on instruments.

"50 Romeo, if you are not efficient in handling instruments, you are going to crash when we direct you down. Are you sure you can handle your plane on instruments with no visual reference?"

One thing I did know was that I was going to have to come down.

"Lexington approach, 50 Romeo. Affirmative. I can handle instruments. I do have over 2000 VFR hours logged."

"50 Romeo, when we get you to a favorable terrain, we will clear the area of traffic and direct you down. We will keep in touch."

Ten miles outside of Lexington, God opened up a hole in the clouds.

"Lexington approach, this is 50 Romeo, I have found a hole. I'll circle down through it."

"50 Romeo, are you sure it is large enough for you?"

"Affirmative," I answered.

"50 Romeo, be sure not to descend below 3,200 feet or you will crash into the hills," they warned.

I circled slowly earthward, watching my instruments, checking my speed, angle of bank, the artificial horizon, staying within the circle, and especially watching my altitude. Within a few minutes I had descended below the clouds, and landed at Lexington, Kentucky, with 20 minutes of gas left.

Before I left my plane, I praised the Lord, and said a prayer of thanksgiving.

After checking into a motel, I went to a nearby restaurant, and ate a good meal. Now you must understand my Christian conviction --- that it is my duty to carry God's message wherever He sends me -- to understand what happened next. On my way out, I noticed two young ladies eating at a table.

"Hi gals, I am Coach Eby from Coldwater, Michigan," I began, introducing myself. "Here is a free copy of a book I wrote for each one of you. The price is right. They cost $2.50 in the bookstores, but I am giving them to you free. Will you take them?" They accepted the books, probably thinking I was some sort of religious eccentric. But I went right ahead.

"If you don't mind, I would like to tell both of you about a new way of life that the book tells about," I offered. "You can turn me off anytime you want to. Isn't that fair enough?" Both girls agreed to listen, by now giving me that what-have-we-got-to-lose look.

About 40 minutes later, both girls accepted Jesus and the new life that He gave them. We left the restaurant together and outside we three joined hands in a circle prayer as I asked our Lord's blessing upon these two new children of God.

As I closed with an amen, I thought this would end the

prayer. But one of the girls, in a special prayer, praised God for detouring me so they could come to know Jesus. God never makes a mistake. He can bring good out of any situation. I sincerely believe this incident at the restaurant, like many others in other places, was part of God's plan for my life of service.

* * *

Arriving home Sunday in Coldwater in time for evening service at my own little church, I found out that six men from Coldwater had crashed in a twin engine plane while landing at the Coldwater airport a few nights earlier. All six had been killed instantly.

I went to their funeral on Monday. All of them were friends of mine. My funeral could have been at the same time, I thought, because I nearly crashed in the mountains of North Carolina on Friday.

My wife Betty has strong faith, but after the death of those six men, and after my close call, she was ready to advertise my plane for sale for ten cents.

Several days later, a lady from Indiana contacted me. "Coach Eby, did you have any particular trouble with your plane last Friday?"

"Yes, sister," I answered. "I almost crashed in the mountains of North Carolina."

"I want you to know," she responded, "that I felt led of the Lord that particular Friday to call a meeting of the ladies of our church. We prayed specifically that God would protect you in that plane as He leads you in traveling in His Ministry."

I am sure happy that I know a Lord who is able and does answer prayers!

* * *

In the third week of July, I took off from the Coldwater airport on a sixteen day speaking and witnessing tour. My first stop was at the Washington, Indiana, airport in southern Indiana. A christian brother picked me up, and drove me to the meeting place.

On the way he informed me, "We don't have a fancy meeting place for you to speak in."

"What does that have to do with it? I could care less where I serve the Lord," I answered.

"In fact," he responded, "you are going to speak in a hog house."

"Do they have the hogs out?" I asked.

He answered my question with an affirmative, and I told him it was alright for me then.

Upon arriving at the hog house, I found it had carpet on the cement floor, christian pictures and plaques on the walls, a small pulpit, and a window air conditioner that just couldn't do the job on this hot, humid July night.

It was a low steel hog house and not too large. However, the Lord really blessed us. About forty adults and twenty teenagers crammed into that meeting place to worship and praise the Lord.

After the meeting I called my friends near Louisville. I asked them to reserve a motel room for me, and to pick me up at the Staniford Airport in Louisville, Kentucky, at midnight. My friend drove me back to the airport. I headed my skyhawk toward Louisville landing there at midnight.

My friends were waiting for me, and drove me to a nearby town where I was going to have meetings the next two days. Arriving at my motel at about one o'clock in the morning, I asked the receptionist for my room reservation.

"I am so very sorry, sir, but all our rooms are rented," she informed me.

"Didn't you have a room reserved for Floyd Eby?" I asked.

"Yes, Sir," she answered, "but I didn't think you were coming because it was so late, and I rented it to another party. It was all my fault, Sir," she continued. "I am very, very sorry."

GOD IS MY PILOT/25

She expected to be "chewed out" in the worst way, and was really dreading it.

"You didn't have anything to do with it," I told her.

"Yes, I did," she answered. "I am completely at fault, and I am sorry."

"I insist," I answered, "that you didn't have anything to do with it. If God had wanted me to stay here tonight, you could not have rented that room. You see my God is powerful and able and knows my future. He didn't want me to stay here tonight or He would have kept a room for me."

"I gave her a copy of my book, "Calling God's Tower, Come in Please," and a Bible. I then left for another motel where I stayed the night. I was able to witness to a person at this new motel.

* * *

After two days of meetings in the Louisville area, I directed my plane to Tulsa, Oklahoma, where I had several meetings and many witnessing opportunities. I spent a couple of hours in one of Tulsa's recreational parks.

In the park, I placed some Bibles and some of my books on a low brick wall where people were continually walking past. Then I started walking in the park looking for someone God would lead me to. I noticed a middleage lady talking to a boy about sixteen years old. I could readily see that they had problems.

"Hi ya, friends," I said. "I am Coach Eby from Coldwater, Michigan. Are you from Tulsa?"

The lady informed me they were from Kansas.

"I have found a new way of life," I continued.

"It is just tremendous. It is free, and it can take away all of your problems." They agreed to listen, and 35 minutes later they professed Jesus and joined the Family of God.

I went back to the brick wall where I had left the Bibles and my books. Two girls were looking and brousing through the Bibles and books.

I spoke loudly to them, "Hey you, those are my books!"
"We weren't going to take them," one of the girls replied.
"We were just looking at them."

"Well, I am going to give them to you free." I caught
them by surprise. They willingly accepted the Bibles and
books, and accepted Christ as I told them about God's Plan
for their lives.

As I went back to the wall there were others whom God
had waiting to talk to me. I talked to twenty people in two
hours. Not one of them objected to me as I talked to them
about the Bible and Jesus. What an exciting time we live in!

* * *

After leaving Tulsa, I was flying over the desert. It was
hot, and I was bucking a 50 mile an hour wind. What a
forsaken area. I thought if my motor stopped, and even if I
survived the emergency landing, I could easily die from thirst
before I could reach a road or find someone.

I then remembered that I had no water on board, not even
in the radiator as my plane's engine was air cooled. Because
of the strong wind, I realized I was never going to reach my
next stop before I ran out of gas.

I started looking for the best place to set down in that hot
desert. Both of my tanks were registering empty when,
praise God, I spotted a small airstrip. I came to a bouncing
stop on my cross wind landing. I located a man who sold me
some gas, and then proceeded on to my next regular stop.

It wasn't long before I was flying over mountains! I
realized this would be much worse than the desert if I had to
make a forced landing. Many of the mountain valleys were
surrounded with high, steep cliffs.

If a person survived a crash, he would certainly have
trouble getting out to civilization. Right then, I praised God
that I had a motor on my plane that never stops. It never
had during the ten years I had owned it.

I landed at Needles, California, a hot and dry place. I

gassed up and took off as soon as possible. Some time later I flew past Palm Springs, and called their tower to let them know I was in their area. I flew down through the pass with high mountains on each side, heading toward Los Angeles. The smog became thick in the pass and visibility was poor. My altitude was 6500 feet above sea level.

"50 Romeo, this is Palm Springs tower. We have a Lear jet taking off to head down through the pass."

"Palm Springs tower, this is 50 Romeo. You notify him that I am at 6500 and to keep his eyes open as he goes by me."

He must have passed me but I never saw him.

I was now in radar contact with Los Angeles approach, and they had me identified on my transponder.

"Los Angeles approach, this is 50 Romeo. I request permission to commence my descent to El Monte airport."

"Descent approved, 50 Romeo," they answered.

I pulled the throttle back and started my descent. Immediately my plane started shaking violently. I soon realized that a valve had gone out. The motor was still running but it had lost most of its power.

I guessed that the El Monte airport was still about 15 miles away. I prayed that I had enough altitude to reach it, and that I would be able to locate it in the smog. I estimated I had less than a mile of visibility in the smog.

"Los Angeles approach, this is 50 Romeo. Give me direction and distance to El Monte airport."

"50 Romeo, this is approach. El Monte is 12 miles at 12 o'clock."

I was anxiously checking how fast I was losing altitude to see if I was going to make it or crash into the streets. The visibility problem was also acute.

I knew I would not see the airport unless I flew directly over it. It certainly was going to be most difficult to stay on the proper course. I knew because of the mountains, I would lose radar contact as soon as I got a little lower.

"Approach, this is 50 Romeo. Give me current direction

and distance to El Monte."

The answer came back like a soft whisper. I could hardly make out the words. It was 4 miles at 12 o'clock.

I now knew I was on my own from here on in. I decided to turn it over to my pilot, God Himself.

"Lord, you know where that airport is, and you can direct this plane directly there. You also know if I don't reach it, this plane is going to crash in the streets. If we miss that airport we will crash in the streets of Los Angeles."

I thought we had missed the airport entirely when I looked down. Praise God, I saw some planes, and immediately radioed the El Monte tower about my power failure. I notified them I was going to dump it down on runway 18, which I did. I could barely taxi it from there.

I spent two days witnessing in this area until my plane was repaired. I then took off for Oregon in the early afternoon, after the smog had lifted. The engine was running hot after the new valve, and the weather was dry and hot.

As the temperature needle reached the red caution line on the gauge, I had second thoughts about flying over the mountains. Many of the mountains were too high for my Skyhawk. I had to go around and between some of them.

I was now particularly suspicious of my engine's reliability, and kept wondering if I could glide to certain valleys if it stopped again. I realized it was going to be next to impossible to make a forced landing anywhere in this area. I decided I was just as safe at night, because I couldn't land anywhere except at an airport. I flew the last three hours over the mountains in the dark and landed at Redmond, Oregon.

After a week of traveling up and down the Pacific coast speaking and witnessing, I headed my Skyhawk back toward Michigan. I ran into thunderstorms and lightning about seventy miles west of Flagstaff, Arizona. Knowing that the turbulence within such thunderstorms could tear my plane apart, I was trying my best to go around them. I kept trying to go around them by going south. But I had not planned to fly as far southward as the storm pushed me. I ended up in Phoenix, where I decided to land and stay the night. The storm came roaring into Phoenix shortly after I landed.

I knew my Lord had a reason, and I found out. I was able to witness to about a dozen people about my Jesus --- people whom I could not have met, had I not landed there.

I left Phoenix the next noon and flew all afternoon and all night until I arrived over Coldwater at 5:30 a.m., making stops only long enough to gas up.

* * *

In the fall I was flying back to Coldwater from Tulsa, Oklahoma, from a series of meetings. It was Sunday afternoon, and the more I flew to the northeast, the worse the weather became. From the weather reports, I knew I could never go all the way to Coldwater that night. I had two of my good friends with me. I told them we would stop and stay overnight in St. Louis, Missouri, and then try to go on home the next day.

As I approached St. Louis, I decided that I would rather stay in a small town. Looking at my chart, I selected a town by the name of Litchfield, Illinois, about 40 miles northeast of St. Louis.

I spoke to my Lord. "Lord, if you give me the weather to get to Litchfield, I promise you that I will land and stay overnight and see what you do with the weather tomorrow. If I can't get to Litchfield, I will turn back and stay at St. Louis."

God was good and I landed at Litchfield without mishap. My friends, Bob and Laura, and I walked to a motel, and checked into our rooms. We then went to a nearby restaurant and ate our evening meal. It was about 9:00 p.m., and there were not many customers in the restaurant. When I finished my meal, I noticed two waitresses visiting at a table with apparently nothing to do.

I stopped and introduced myself, and gave each one a

book and a Bible. I started to talk to them about this wonderful new way of life. The girls were listening intently when four more families came in to be served.

I believe it is dishonest to talk to people when they are supposed to be working. I left the books and Bibles with them, and walked back to my motel room.

All the way back I was praising God. No one except my wife, Bob, and Laura know where I am, I thought. There will be no phone calls or interruptions. I can do just as I please: read the paper, pray, read the Bible, watch television, and sleep until noon. The weather was forecast to be bad until afternoon.

I went to bed at 10:30 p.m. I had only been in bed two minutes when there was a knock on the door.

"Is Coach Eby in there?"

I thought to myself, "Who could this be anyway? No one knows I'm here except Bob and Laura, and it is not Bob's voice."

I asked, "What do you want?"

"I am a truck driver," he replied, "and I need to see you."

I shouted back to him, "Just a minute, please." I climbed out of bed and went to the door and opened it. There, standing in the doorway, was a man about 40 years old.

He started apologizing to me for waking me so late at night, but he said he just had to see me.

"Don't apologize. Come on in. I have been expecting you," I told him.

"What do you mean?" he answered, "You don't even know me."

"That doesn't make any difference," I replied. "I have been expecting you."

"How come?" he asked.

"Because I was flying my plane back to Coldwater, Michigan, from Tulsa, Oklahoma, and God blocked the flight with weather and there was no way I could get back to Coldwater. I was going to land at St. Louis and stay overnight, and some way God led me to stay overnight at

Litchfield. I have never been here before in my life. I just know that God had a reason for me being here tonight. And you are the first reason to show up, so come on in!"

"I wasn't supposed to be here either," he replied. "According to my trucking firm regulations, I was supposed to sleep in Chicago tonight. I had so many problems that I couldn't sleep so I got in my truck and drove 200 miles. I was in the restaurant getting a cup of coffee when I saw you talking to those waitresses. I said to myself, that man is really happy. I wish I was happy like that but I can't be because I have too many problems. When you walked out of the restaurant, I went to one of the waitresses, and she let me look at your book. I decided that I had to talk with you. I located the motel you were staying in, and got your room number from the office, and here I am."

"Sit down," I said as I showed him to a chair.

He sat down and replied, "It is going to take a long time for me to tell you about all my problems."

"I don't want to hear them," I replied.

"Why not?" he asked.

"Because I can't help you with your problems," I emphasized.

I went over to the motel dresser and picked up the Gideon placed Bible, and came back to Dick.

"However, Dick, if you want to listen, I will tell you about someone who can help you with your problems. Are you willing to listen?" He said he was.

We spent at least an hour in the Word of God. I told Dick about God's Wonderful Plan for his life. Dick accepted Jesus and joined the Family of God. He hugged me as I prayed with him. Tears appeared on his face, as he went out that motel door a new creature in Christ. As he drove away in his truck, I praised God for a new brother in Christ!

A week after arriving home I wrote Dick a letter as I always do after telling someone about Jesus. Two weeks later, I received an answer from Dick's wife, Barb. Barb said she had been a Christian for ten years. She praised God that

I took the time and had the compassion to show Dick this new way of life.

I had to write and tell Barb, "I regret to inform you," I wrote, "that I didn't have a thing to do with it. You see, Barb, there was no way I could have been in any place but in that motel room at that time. This was a pre-arranged meeting between me, Dick, and the Holy Spirit. I was just fortunate to be in God's Will when He answered your prayers. I know this is true, Barb, as we serve a great God, one that never makes a mistake."

I now have Dick's family picture on my prayer board, and I pray for them regularly.

* * *

Just before departing for Port Huron, Michigan, one day, I, as usual, called the weatherman at the Jackson Flight Service Station. They reported marginal VFR with widely scattered thunderstorms. As I approached Jackson, I called the Flight Service again to see if the report had been amended.

"Jackson Radio, this is Cessna 5750 Romeo. What is your latest report on weather between Jackson and Port Huron."

"50 Romeo, this is Jackson. You picked a lousy day. A bad thunderstorm went through Jackson about an hour ago, and is now in your path in the Ann Arbor area. There are additional storms scattered all over this area."

"Jackson Radio, 50 Romeo. If I get into trouble, what would be the best direction of flight to get out of it?"

"50 Romeo," they answered, "If you insist on flying in such conditions as this, we can be of no help. You are strictly on your own."

That's what he thinks, I thought. I know better because I have the best help there is. I have my Lord as my pilot. I am the co-pilot.

"Lord, I am going to steer a course directly to Port Huron. If you want me to go around a storm, you show me the way and when. If you want me safely in Port Huron for tonight's meeting, then you supply the safe pathway."

I set my course on a straight line to Port Huron.

I passed thunderstorms on either side practically the entire way, but I never changed course one degree, and never ran into any part of any storm. I landed at Port Huron, and asked the attendant to gas up my plane, and push it into their large hangar. I told him to be sure that my plane went last into the hangar so I could go home about 11:00 p.m. if the weather was OK. He promised me he would take care of it.

After the meeting my friend brought me to the airport, and the weather was becoming worse by the minute, with lightning, thunder, wind, and rain. I called the weatherman. After his report, I decided that I could fly north to Saginaw, and circle around to a northerly direction and end up at Coldwater.

My friend and I grabbed my luggage and ran through the rain to the large hangar with the door open. I expected my plane to be the first one inside the door. It was clear in the back with at least six planes ahead of it.

"Thank you, Lord," I meditated, "You made the answer for me. There is no way that I can go home now."

God proved Himself once again as I was led to witness to several that night and the next morning.

* * *

After two morning services at two different churches in Muskegon, Michigan one Sunday, I was driven to the airport to fly my plane home. During the last hour the weather had turned sour, the ceiling was low, and the fog had cut the visibility to a critical range. I just knew there was no chance that the tower would allow a VFR pilot to leave under those circumstances.

However, I climbed in my plane and called the tower.

"Muskegon Tower, this is Cessna 5750 Romeo parked here on the ramp. What is the current weather in Grand Rapids?"

The tower informed me that Grand Rapids was OK at the present, but it was going to be bad in ten minutes. Just for fun, I was going to give the Muskegon Tower a chance to refuse me permission to depart.

"Muskegon Tower. 50 Romeo. I request a special VFR to depart for Coldwater, Michigan."

"Affirmative, 50 Romeo," they answered.

I didn't believe my ears. "Tower, 50 Romeo. Did you say negative?"

The tower reaffirmed that they had granted my request. Even though I knew better, I was considering leaving on radar and instruments, thinking that within ten minutes I would be in decent weather.

Just as I was ready to request taxiing instructions, a United Airlines jet buzzed the runway at about two hundred feet. I immediately stepped out of my plane. I went into the terminal building, and asked the United Airlines counter what happened to their jet that was coming in. He informed me that the pilot had decided that the weather was too bad to land and he went back to Chicago.

That settled it for me. If all their pilots with all their know-how and instruments would not land in this weather, then my Skyhawk was going to stay on the ground. I stayed overnight.

*"He who has said all these things
declares: Yes, I am coming soon!
Amen! Come, Lord Jesus!"*
Revelation 22:20

2

TIME IS RUNNING OUT

Nothing To Live For

I was serving the Lord in Texas for an extended time when I received an emergency call from Houston. A tragedy had struck a family.

I didn't know the family but a Christian friend asked me if I would fly to Houston. I jumped into my plane and landed at one of the small Houston airports. My friend picked me up and drove me to a hospital where Carol, a high school student, was in a coma.

Carol had been depressed and under the care of a psychiatrist. After one of the sessions, the psychiatrist called the parents. "Mr. and Mrs. Smith, I don't trust Carol. She is very despondent. I recommend   that you keep a close eye on her for the next several days." Carol's father moved to a different bedroom so her mother, Beulah, could have Carol with her.

During the night as Beulah awakened, she noticed that Carol was not in bed. Beulah immediately got up. She found the basement door opened. As she went to the basement, she found Carol swinging from a rope.

Beulah and her husband cut her down and rushed her to the hospital. Carol was still alive but in a coma. Her sister, also a high school student, went berserk. She kept saying that if Carol died, she was going to kill herself too. It just seemed too much for Sally to stand.

When I arrived at the hospital, I was ushered into Carol's room. She was still in a coma and remained unconscious and passed away the next day. I was unable to talk with the parents, Beulah and Leroy, because they were busy making arrangements to get Sally to the psychiatrist.

I talked to four relatives about the Bible and Jesus. During that session I learned that there had not been much love shown in the family. The love of Jesus was not known. Both girls had found what youth seemed to be looking for --- dope, alcohol, and sex. According to the world, they had everything, but now there was nothing to live for.

I thought to myself, what a clear illustration of today's world. Everything without Jesus is nothing. We just can't make it in this world successfully without Jesus in our lives. We can put on a good front. We can appear happy, but there just can't be real joy without Jesus! The devil can give us fun, but only Jesus can give us joy. Fun is only temporary, but joy is lasting.

After the death of her sister, Carol, Sally turned rebellious, hateful, and suicidal. She didn't want to talk with anyone. Beulah, the mother, believed in God, but her belief wasn't working for her. Leroy, the father, was an atheist.

After my one trip to the Houston hospital, I made no further attempt to contact the family. I just prayed for the family --- especially Sally. I also knew that some of the close relatives who were Christians were also praying. I felt if God wanted me to follow up on this family, He would have the family contact me.

TIME IS RUNNING OUT/37

Several weeks later, I received a letter from Beulah. She wanted to know if I would come to Houston and talk with the family. I wrote back and told her I would be happy to talk to any member of the family who wanted to talk with me. However, I would not talk to anyone who didn't want to talk to me, including Sally.

One day as I was writing in my motel room, I felt led to call Beulah to see if she had received my letter. Someone answered the phone and told me that Beulah was not there.

"Who is this?" I asked.

"This is Sally," was the answer.

Sally was the last one I wanted to talk to. But now I was stuck.

"Sally, you don't know me and I don't know you, but I am Coach Eby."

"Coach Eby, I know about you. I am reading your book. I have questions to ask you. I want to talk with you. Will you come see me? You made my day by calling."

I praise God that He really answers prayers. I now knew that He had already prepared Sally's heart and she was ready to receive Jesus. I set up an appointment for two weeks later to meet Sally at a Houston airport.

I took Sally flying and made friends with her. Then Beulah, Sally, and I went to their home. Both Sally and her mother accepted Jesus. I just know that our Lord will now pull them through. I also believe our prayers will change and prepare Leroy, the father. I praise God for this family. They mean so much to me. I just love all of them!

There You Are, You Can Have Them

I was scheduled to speak at a large country church in northern Michigan, on a Sunday night. The church was packed. I slipped into the church and located an empty pew next to a young lady. After sitting there for a few minutes and being bathed in the warmth of the Holy Spirit, I leaned over and whispered to the young lady.

"Sister, I really feel the presence of the Holy Spirit among this group tonight, and I believe something great is going to happen --- tonight."

She whispered back, "Brother, I sincerely believe you are right."

As I was giving the message, I just knew that God was moving among many of us. At the end of the message, I gave an invitation.

"If God has been speaking to you tonight, and you want to get right with God, you may come to the altar, or go into the room on the left, or stay in the back of the church, or give me your address or phone number."

I closed with a short prayer, and turned the meeting over to the local Pastor. As he made some concluding comments, I walked to the rear of the sanctuary.

When the Pastor said "Amen" at the end of a short concluding prayer, a tall teenager broke from the pew and started down the aisle in rapid long strides. However, he wasn't headed toward the altar but to the back and to the outdoors. His short buddy was following him, and with his short legs he had to run to keep up.

As they approached the back, I stepped right out in front of them, held up my hand and demanded, "Stop. No one is going to get out of this church until I shake hands with them."

They shook hands, smiling, saying they were Chad and Jerry. They then hustled out of the church. In three minutes, Chad came back in and threw a pack of cigarettes at me.

"There you are. You can have them. I am going to the altar."

Chad rushed down the aisle to the altar with his long rapid strides. Jerry once again had to run to keep up. Both of them went to their knees at the altar and talked with God.

God is good. Twenty-four more besides Chad and Jerry talked with me that night and got right with God. It was after midnight before I was able to fly my Skyhawk home.

TIME IS RUNNING OUT/39

And this testimony does not end here.

Several weeks later when I arrived home from two weeks of meetings, my wife had a message for me. "A lady up north called and wanted you to know that Jerry, the short buddy of Chad, who followed Chad to the altar that Sunday night, was killed in an automobile accident. I am sure that Coach Eby would want to know."

When my wife told me, I just said Praise the Lord. I also praised the Lord for Chad. Not only did he get right with God that night, he had set the example for Jerry. I believe that if Chad hadn't moved that night when God spoke to him, Jerry, his buddy wouldn't have either. Chad's buddy, Jerry, could have gone into a Christless Eternity.

Friends, we not only need to get right with God because of our own needs, but we all have other friends who are waiting for us to lead the way. What a responsibility we have!

He's Not Ready Yet

I didn't know Dee before she called me one day.

"I know we don't know each other, but I have a problem. I am at the hospital, and my father is here and he is dying with cancer. I have read your book and I don't understand about these things. However, I do realize that whatever happens after death, he's not ready yet. Would you please come down here?"

Upon arriving at the hospital, I found many of Don's relatives and friends in his room. I introduced myself, and then asked Don's wife if she would have everyone go to the reception room if she wanted me to speak to her husband. They all left.

Don was very feeble, and appeared to be near death.

"Don, do you realize you are very ill?" He answered yes.

"Don, do you believe in God?"

"In sort of a way," he replied.

"Do you believe in the Bible, Don?"

"In sort of a way," he whispered.

A son and Dad united by Jesus.

Apparently Don didn't believe and wasn't really interested. Normally, I just leave when I receive this type of reaction. But seeing Don near death, I had to make sure that I recognized God's open door if it was there.

I talked a few minutes more and the Holy Spirit took over. Don accepted Jesus and I then prayed with him. I went to the reception room and announced to the relatives that my brother Don was right with God, and that his future had been guaranteed through God's Precious Word!

Three days later, Dee called me and told me that Don had passed away.

"Coach, even though our family doesn't know you too well, we would all like to have you give the funeral message."

I checked my calendar and agreed. As I visited with the family at the funeral home, I was able to make friends.

Dee said, "Coach we are burying that little brown testament you gave Dad with him. He had us help him sign his name in the back where he recorded the results of your visit. Dad thought so much of this brown testament. He talked about it often, and told us how he had accepted Jesus."

After the funeral, Dee and her husband and two other relatives asked me to come to their home and talk with them. All four of them accepted Jesus and joined the Family of God.

God Knows Best

Brother Jerry had been saved for three years. He had a good personality and people loved him. He had a great influence for Jesus especially among young people. Jerry and I were very close. We believed and thought alike. We enjoyed witnessing to other people. Jerry would also pick up hitch-hikers, work in jails, witness in his business, and on the streets.

I felt possibly that the Lord would eventually have Jerry take over the Ministry that He had given me. Jerry asked me to pray that the Lord would give him a different job that would leave more time for God's Work. Jerry went with me quite often and gave his testimony.

I really loved this brother, but our Lord took him home at the age of twenty-five through an accident. It seemed to leave a void in my life, but I know our Lord knows best. I must try not to run ahead of my Lord!

I Am Not Ready To Accept Jesus

I was speaking to a large group of men at a noon luncheon in a Michigan city. I knew that most of them had to go back to work, and would be leaving in a hurry. After closing in prayer, I immediately went to the back door so I could shake hands and meet each one as they left. One man shook my hand and handed me a business card. He asked me to call him, and then left in a hurry.

A couple of the men stayed until everyone else was gone. They had seen the man hand me his card, and they wanted to make sure I would contact him. "He is a well known realtor in this city; he is financially well-off, but he needs Jesus," one of the men said. "We have been inviting him to these meetings for two years. Once in a while he sends one of his salesmen, but he never came himself, until today. This is the first time he has ever come. We watched him during the meeting and we believe God was speaking to him."

I assured them that I would follow up on Ron.

I called Ron late that night after I arrived home.

"Ron, this is Coach Eby, you asked me to call you. What can I do for you?"

"Coach, I am ashamed to admit it but I have been drinking. I want you to know that God spoke to me this noon as you were giving the message. My life is in a mess, and I don't know what to do. I need to talk with you sometime."

The word "sometime" is of the devil. The word never sets an appointment.

"Ron, this is Thursday night. The first available time I have is Monday. How about then?"

"Coach, I will meet you anytime or any place; you just name it. I will drive all the way to your home."

"Ron, I have business in a city near your home on Monday. What about meeting me at the airport at 1:30 in the afternoon."

"I will be there," Ron promised.

I flew my Skyhawk into the airport of the designated city at 1:30 p.m. As I got out of my plane, Ron drove up in his eighteen thousand dollar car. We sat in his car to have our session.

"Coach, I just don't know what to do. My life is falling

apart. My wife has left me, and I am drinking too much. It is even affecting my business. When I heard you speak, I knew you had something that I need."

"Ron, the answer is Jesus Christ."

"Coach, I am not ready to accept Jesus. I have too many things in my life to change before I can accept Jesus."

"Wait a minute Ron. You are putting the cart before the horse. Your life will never change for the better until you do accept Jesus. Ron, you are destined to failure if you try to run your own life without Jesus. I know because I have tried it. Many thousands of other people I have talked to have also found this true. Ron, you give your life to Jesus and put Him first in your life, and He will take care of all of your problems."

I opened up the Bible and showed Ron God's plan for his life. He accepted Jesus, and I prayed with him before we separated.

I wrote him a personal letter, sent him a Bible course, and called a personal Christian friend in Ron's home city. The friend promised me he would make himself available to encourage Ron to get into a weekly Bible Study and into church activities.

Don't "bug" Him, Love Him

I stopped at a local restaurant and two waitresses that were in my midnight Bible Study called me into the office. We were the only people in the office at the time.

"Coach Eby, we have a problem," one of the waitresses said. "Brad, who works here, is running into trouble. He's on dope and he's drinking heavily. We just know he is going to get in trouble. We like him and we want to help him. We tried talking to him about Jesus and we've invited him to our Bible Study. But he claims that he doesn't believe in a God. What do we do now?"

"Connie and Jill, if Brad doesn't believe there is a God, there is no use talking to him about spiritual things. Just try to make friends with him."

"Coach, we really don't believe that he means what he says about no God."

"Girls, you have to take him at his word. Just make friends with him. Pray for him even when you don't want to. Get as close to God as you possibly can yourself. He is watching you. Don't bug him. Just love him."

Connie and Jill must have done a lot of praying. Brad came to the midnight Bible Study that very night for the first time. He sat on the floor right across from me. I changed my lesson in a hurry, and went through salvation. Brad listened attentively and joined hands with us during the closing prayer.

I was disappointed. The next Wednesday night, Brad wasn't there at the Bible Study. As we closed in prayer I asked for prayer requests. Connie asked us to pray for Brad. Just that morning Brad had been in a terrible automobile accident. He was in a Battle Creek hospital, and was not expected to live. We prayed for him, and committed him to God.

The next morning I called the hospital, and asked how Brad was. The nurse told me that during the night Brad had taken a definite turn for the better, and this morning he was no longer on the critical list. Praise the Lord!

I told the hospital that I was a spiritual counselor, and I had a meeting in Battle Creek that night. I wanted to know if it would be possible for me to see Brad about 9:00 p.m. They told me to stop in and they would let me know at that time.

When I arrived at the hospital, I had to wait some time to see Brad. His girlfriend, whom I knew and who was my sister in Christ, wanted to go in to see Brad at the same time. The nurse said it would be OK.

I introduced myself to another young lady who was waiting. She was still another friend of Brad's.

While we were waiting, I talked to Brad's friend about Jesus, and she accepted Him just before we went into Brad's room.

Brad was in bad shape. A mass of splints, bandages, and tubes. He could not open his mouth. Brad's girl friend, Pat, stood on one side of the bed and I on the other. Pat held one of his hands and I held the other. I asked Brad if he could hear us all right and he squeezed my hand.

I asked Brad to answer my question, yes by squeezing my hand, and to answer no by not squeezing my hand.

"Do you understand?" He squeezed my hand.

I opened up the Bible and told Brad about Jesus. Brad accepted each step of salvation by squeezing my hand and also Pat's hand. Each time, Pat would look over to me and smile. Brad accepted Jesus and joined the Family of God by just answering yes to God.

The doctors claimed that Brad would be in the hospital for weeks, and it would be months before he could walk again. Two weeks later he was at our midnight Bible Study. He walked in under his own power with crutches.

When we closed the Bible study with a circle prayer, we asked those who didn't want to pray to just squeeze the next person's hand; those who wanted to pray were to do so.

When Brad's turn came he prayed thanking God. He also prayed for a six year old girl in his home town who had been struck by a car. I praise God for the prayers and encouragement of Connie and Jill in Brad's behalf.

Why Does God Allow This To Happen To Me?

A lady realtor closed a house deal for me in a nearby city, and in order to save time with the paperwork I asked Donna to meet me at the airport. She brought her salesman with her. The salesman asked me about my work. I gave him a copy of my book and a Bible, and I told him about this new way of life. He joined the Family of God. Donna said she was already a Christian.

Two weeks later, Donna called me.

"Coach Eby, I need to see you. Would you spare me some

of your valuable time if I drive over to your home?"

I told her how to get to my home, and she said it would take her an hour and a half.

Down in my recreation room, Donna told me her problems.

"Coach, I know I am a Christian. I love the Lord. I go to church regularly. I pray often. But everything is getting worse every day. Nearly every sale is falling through. I cannot make the payments on my office building I am buying. I am going to lose the building. I am going to lose the business. I am going to lose everything!"

God brought happiness in spite of tragedy.

"Donna, she is no fool who gives up what she cannot keep to gain what she cannot lose!"

"But Coach, why do I have to give up everything I need?"

"Donna, are you trying to run your business and straighten out your life? Why don't you commit it to the Lord and place it in His Hands."

TIME IS RUNNING OUT/47

"Come on Coach, let us be practical. I need to make money to pay the bills."

"Let me ask you some questions, Donna. How much Bible reading do you do each day?"

"Very little Coach. I just don't have time. You know how the real estate business is - a continual business."

"In your prayer life, Donna, are you spending most of the prayers on yourself and your business?"

She confirmed it.

"Donna, did you every try spending most of your prayer time praising God for what He has done and praying for other people? Donna, how much time each day do you spend serving Jesus?"

"I just don't have the time, Coach. I just don't have the time. It just isn't possible to have much time to serve Jesus."

"Donna, do you expect God to prosper your business if you don't spend time in His Word. You don't spend time praising Him and praying for others. You don't spend time serving Him. No way, Donna. You are mocking our Lord Jesus. Listen to this verse, Donna. *Galatians 6:7 Be not deceived; God is not mocked: for whatsoever a man soweth, that shall he also reap.*

Donna is doing much better in all ways since she is pleasing God!

Passing from death unto life
or
Passing from death unto torture

During a church crusade I was asked to visit an elderly couple out in the country. The man was seriously ill and his wife had to take care of him twenty-four hours a day. Neither one of them knew Jesus.

I knocked on the door and Mildred opened it. She asked me what I wanted.

"I am Coach Eby and I am having a church crusade in this area," I said. "Some friends of yours asked me to stop and visit with you. Could I say hello to Bill?"

Mildred asked me to come in, and led me into the room where Bill was resting in a chair, asleep. Mildred tried to wake him but couldn't.

"Don't bother him, Mildred," I suggested. "What about me coming back at 5:00 p.m.?" Mildred indicated that she thought that would be better.

Mildred let me back in at 5:00 p.m. and I introduced myself to Bill. He was obviously very ill with not much time left. Although he surveyed me with much suspicion and coldness, I was able to make friends with both him and his wife.

With Bill's and Mildred's permission, I took out my Bible and told them about Jesus. After talking with them for about twenty minutes, Bill interrupted me. "Coach, you will have to excuse me, but I can sit in this chair only so long. I now have to be moved back into the bed."

"Would you like to have me leave, Bill?" I asked.

"No," he answered, "I want to hear the rest of it."

Mildred declined my offer to help her move him back to the bed. She went through certain procedures indicating that she had done this many times before.

After Bill was resting in the bed I continued with God's plan for their lives. He and Mildred both accepted Jesus. We had a circle prayer holding hands around that sick bed.

After the prayer, I told Bill, "You have now passed from death unto life. You are now in God's Hands, and He has guaranteed your future as well as Mildred's."

They were pleased and excited, and they asked me to come back any time I could. I visited Bill and Mildred the next day, wrote them a letter, sent a Bible Course, and asked some of my Christian friends to make calls on a regular basis.

Soon after in an adjacent community, a lady asked me to visit her husband who was dying of emphysema. She was a Christian but her husband wasn't. She was concerned about him going into a Christless Eternity.

I tried to make friends with Jim, but without much success. I tried to talk with him about the future through Jesus. Jim didn't seem interested.

"Jim, do you want me to talk to you about God's plan for your life?"

"Not really," he answered. "I am not interested in the future, just in the present, day by day. You know that I am not going to get any better with this disease. It is going to get worse each day until I die. There is no help for me. I don't care about the future. I am just interested in this pain I am having right now. The future can take care of itself."

"Jim, you would rather have me leave, wouldn't you?"

"That's right," he answered.

I left but stopped on the porch to tell his grief-stricken wife that Jim at the present was not interested in the help of Jesus. I suggested she keep praying for him, keep getting close to God herself, and not to "bug" him but love him.

My first friend, Bill chose life and happiness in Jesus, but my second friend, Jim, chose death and torture. I don't know why, but I do know that we all have a free choice. That is God's Way!

And God shall wipe away all tears
from their eyes; and there shall
be no more death, neither sorrow,
nor crying, neither shall there
be any more pain: for the former
things are passed away.
Revelation 21:4

3

OUR FUTURE LIFE GUARANTEED

My Own Testimony

Two brothers, a sister, and I were raised on a farm by my Christian parents, Jesse and Marcia Eby. Materially, we were a poor family. I resented this proverty and the fact that I had to go without many things my friends had. Although my parents were Christians, I was not. I vowed that I was going to be concerned about obtaining desirable things for myself. I wanted to be a coach, a teacher, a sports announcer, a pilot, and to make money.

I praise God that I lived in a country where a nobody like me could come off a farm and in a few short years obtain all the goals I desired. However, for many years I lacked the one really important ingredient for complete happiness: *a personal encounter with the Lord Jesus!*

Although I had heard hundreds of sermons and Sunday school lessons, I had never really joined the Family of God.

My mother was sick for ten years when I was a small boy and a young teenager. I prayed on my knees each night that God would make my mother well. He never did, and I hated God for that! My mother passed away when I was a freshman at college.

For many years, my interest was in playing and coaching sports, teaching, airplanes, making money, and becoming prominent and popular. I went to church, and I taught Sunday school classes. But I wasn't really too interested in spiritual things. I thought I was a Christian headed toward Heaven because of the good life I was living, in serving my community and helping young people.

During World War II, as a Communication Officer overseas on a Destroyer Escort, I started reading the Bible and found that I was a lost sinner in spite of my goodness. And I knew that I was outside the protection of God.

However, in attempting to make the Bible practical, and to prove it, I became a confused young man. Finally, one day I decided to either become an atheist, and throw out all this religious nonsense, or accept God for what He says He is! Right then, I decided to accept each word of God as truth by faith that God is no liar. I have not been confused since.

However, for years I grew very slowly spiritually. I did not consistently do the things needed to grow close to God. I read the Bible occasionally and went to church. But I did not discipline myself to be consistent in Bible reading, praying, being with other Christians, and serving Jesus.

I was making more money than ever before. One day my Lord shook me up: *Galatians 6:7 "Be not deceived, God is not mocked; for whatsoever a man soweth, that shall he also reap."*

I lost $40,000.00 in two business deals within three days, and immediately I asked my Lord, "Why me?" I reminded my Lord that I had been going to church regularly, teaching Sunday school class and giving thousands of dollars each year to my church and other missionaries.

My Lord answered me quickly, "Don't give me any more

While receiving a high school education, she found a new life in Christ.

jazz about that money you are giving me. I want your dedication, time and talent."

Right then, I surrendered my life, time, talent, and money to my Saviour. I have been richly blessed ever since. Each day with Jesus is sweeter than the day before!

Four Reasons Why I Believe and Know The Bible Is True

The following four reasons are why I believe and know the Bible is true. They really make sense to me now. I pray they will also make sense to you, as belief in the Bible is the key to this wonderful way of life I am telling you about.

The first reason I believe the Bible is true is the fulfilling of prophecies. You see, being a scientist, I believed in science, not the Bible. I now completely believe the Bible. Some top scientists are personal friends of mine, and they too at one time were agnostics or atheists, believing only science and not the Bible. Dr. John Moore from Michigan State University was an avowed agnostic until 1962. He believed in only science, and thought God, Jesus, and the Bible were nonsense as I did. In 1962, Dr. Moore became a Christian, and three years later in 1965, he was speaking to a group of men about the harmony of the Bible and science. By that time I believed the Bible, and I had taught science for many years. I drove up to Michigan State University to hear him.

Dr. Moore used two illustrations that day that I still remember. "At one time," he said, "Science had established the fact that there were just 1,054 stars in the Universe." May I ask you readers if you ever tried counting the stars on a clear night? Well, I have, and I have found out that when you get up to 15 or 20 stars, you become confused and mixed up and cannot keep track. I have also attempted to count them while in a planetarium where I used to teach about the sun, moon, and stars. It couldn't be done there either.

So, the scientists found they couldn't count the stars. They had collaborated and went to their experts; the books and charts ... and established the scientific fact of 1,054 stars in the Universe, no more and no less.

But while we scientists had established this fact, God's Word had already recorded in Genesis 15:5 that God compared the number of stars with the seed of people, or millions of people. Also, in Hebrew 11:12, God compared the number of stars with the grains of sand at the seashore. Did you ever try to count the grains of sand when you were swimming on a sandy beach?

You see, friends, when science had established the fact of 1,054 stars, God's Word had already recorded that the stars were too numerous to be counted, and now science agrees with the Bible on this.

Dr. Moore also stated that at one time, science had

established the fact that the earth was hung in place by cables. Of course, we laugh at that now, because we know that we place things in orbit and around and around they go with nothing attached thereto. Science at that time knew about gravity, but not about space, so science just knew that the earth had to be hooked to something, or it would fall out of space. After talking with the experts --- checking their books and charts --- we scientists decided that it was a fact that the Earth was hung in space by cables.

However, as we go to Job 26:7 we read that God hangeth the earth up on nothing. God's Word is continuing to prove scientific facts as wrong, and the only time that the Bible and science disagree is when science is wrong! Praise God!

The second reason I believe the Bible, and know that it is true, is because it changes people's lives.

Yes, I was one of those people who used to ridicule matured Christians.

"Look at that religious nut. He has gone nuts on religion. He is a fanatic. He is way out in left field. They ought to lock him up and throw away the key. Man -- is he gone!" I used to say.

However, no matter how much I ridiculed the Christians, in my own mind, I had to admit that something was changing their lives, even though the way He was changing them was distasteful to me at the time. Then when God came in and changed my life and thousands of my friends' lives, I knew it was for real. So it makes sense that the Bible is true if it has the power to change lives.

The third reason I believe the Bible, and know that it is true, is because God is no liar. When I was overseas I had to make a decision, as I asked myself this question. "Is God the greatest liar ever created, the greatest phony ever produced, the greatest fake ever brought about -- or does He tell the truth and is He what He claims to be?"

You see God is not like Floyd Eby. I tell the truth most of the time and sometimes I lie. But God is either what He claims He is, or He is the greatest liar ever created.

I decided right then and there that *God is no liar*. From the point of starting, I now could make a simple scientific deduction. If God is no liar, then He tells the truth. If He tells the truth, then God said He wrote the Bible, then it has to all be true, because God only tells the truth. I believe that there can be a few errors in some translations, but I know there is not one error in the original writings, as God wrote it.

In *II Peter 1:20-21* we read, *"Knowing this first, that no prophecy of the scripture is of any private interpretation. For the prophecy came not at any time by the will of man, but holy men of God spoke as they were moved by the Holy Spirit."* If you wished to write a book and asked me to type it as you dictated to me, and I typed every word just as you told it to me, who would be the author of the book, you or me? You, of course. I was only the typist. You were the author and you understood everything that you wrote even though someone else might read your book and misunderstand some parts of it.

I believe this is the way that God's Book was written. God told these Holy Men of God just what to put down. In other words, these Holy Men of God --- John, Paul, Peter and all the others -- had no choice but to write down exactly what God spoke to them through His Holy Spirit. If I say that God didn't write the Bible in this way, then I am calling Him a liar, because He said He did.

I used to say that I thought parts of the Bible were true, but other parts were not or could not be. However, this same God who cannot lie and wrote the Bible states in *II Timothy 3:16, "All scripture is given by inspiration of God, and is profitable for doctrine, for reproof, for correction, for instruction in righteousness."*

God said, "I wrote it all." The Bible in the original writing has to be true, or none of it is true, because God wrote all of it.

The key to our salvation, our faith, our blessings, and all of God's Promises, are wrapped up in the *fact* that God is no liar. Therefore He tells the truth. Therefore He wrote the Bible. Therefore the Bible has to be true, and we can only rely on His Word for salvation, faith, blessings, and all of God's promises.

The fourth reason I believe the Bible and know that it is true, is that I accept by faith that which I cannot understand.

As you read this, I know many of you are saying to yourself, "Not me, I want everything proven to me." I could prove everything in the Bible to you if only I could place myself on the same intellectual level as God Almighty who wrote the Book. Of course, this is impossible, so I need to accept the parts of the Bible I cannot understand by Faith, because God said it.

I personally fought this concept for years. I am a scientist, a coach, and a teacher, and I wanted all things proven to me as facts. As I diagrammed new football plays, and every man did his job and blocked his man, we would run for a touchdown every play. But we seldom did, because someone was "goofing off," and would miss his man. But I realize that we use faith in our daily living.

One morning one of my high school students came to me in the hall. "Coach Eby, I have some questions to ask you," she said.

"Wait until you come to my first hour class, Sally," I replied, "and we will discuss your questions then."

When the class started, and I gave the students a reading assignment, I took Sally into my adjacent office, and asked her what I could do to help her. She handed me a sheet of questions, and I quickly looked at them and found the questions to be all anti-God and anti-Christian.

"Did you make up these questions, Sally?'"

"No," came the answer, "I got them from my boyfriend at the University."

I thought to myself, this is about "par" for the course.

"This is Friday," I said. "Let me take your questions home over the weekend, and I will look up the answers in God's Word."

The next Monday morning in the hallway, Sally asked if I had the answers to her questions, and I told her I would see her in class. Once again I took her to my office.

"Yes, Sally," I said, "I have some answers to your questions, but you are not going to be satisfied with them."

"Why not?" she asked.

"Because you don't accept the Bible as true and God's Word."

I took the Bible from my desk and held it up. "We must accept the parts of the Bible we can't understand by faith, because God said it."

Sally struck the desk with her fist, and indignantly replied, "You are just like the rest of them. I thought you could help me but you're just like the others, expecting me to accept the Bible on blind faith. I just won't do that because I am not that type of person."

"I am sorry, Sally, that you don't live with your mother," I mentioned.

"But I do," she said.

"No, you don't," I replied.

"Yes, I do."

"No, you don't."

"Yes, I do. You know I do, Coach. You have been to my home and I have introduced you to my mother."

"I regret to inform you, Sally, that is not your real mother. I think you got mixed up in the hospital and were sent to the wrong home."

"I know better than that," Sally protested.

"How do you know, Sally? Did you ever have a blood test? Even that would not prove it for sure."

By now Sally was somewhat confused, and I said to her, "Sure, Sally, you know she is your mother and I know she is your mother, but only through faith that we accept."

Sally saw the point.

Once in a while my teenage daughter would act nasty at home, and sometimes I would say to her, "You know, you are no daughter of mine. My daughter would not act like that. You must have been mixed up in the hospital, and sent to the wrong home." Her mother would answer, "She acts just like her dad."

If I asked you readers who the first President of the United States was, most of you would tell me George Washington. I buy that. In fact, if someone today were able to prove to me that George Washington wasn't the first President of the United States, I would be disturbed. All my life I have known that Washington was the first President.

Traveling through high school and college now with Jesus at her side.

I wasn't there, and I can't prove it but I believe it. I read it in history books. I would like to ask you the question, "Does it make sense to believe without a shadow of a doubt, a history book written by men and women, accepting George Washington as the first President of the United States and many other historical events, and not believe a book (the Bible) written by God? I am sure your answer is, that if we are to accept history books by faith, we must accept the Bible by Faith!

In summary, I believe that the Bible is true, because of the fulfilling of prophecies; because it changes peoples' lives; because God is no liar, and He said He wrote the Bible, and because I accept those parts of the Bible I cannot understand by faith because God said it.

This makes sense to me and I am sure it does to you. If it does make sense to you, then the scriptures can show you as they showed me, the way to join the Family of God.

God Shows The Way

Since we now believe and know that the Bible is true, God will show us through four verses of scripture how to join the Family of God. The first verse is *Romans 3:23*. *"For all have sinned, and come short of the Glory of God."*

For many years I have thought this verse included everyone except Floyd Eby. One day I realized that the "all" in the English language means everybody but Jesus, and that includes all evangelists, all preachers, all men, all women, all children, and most of all, it included me.

You see, I don't know one bad thing about you and you don't know anything bad about me, because we don't know each other. But as you read this book, you know that Floyd Eby does some wrong. You know that much without even knowing me, because God says in this verse that all do wrong, and that not only has to include me but you, too.

Therefore, you and I are in the same boat. We both do wrong and we need help. In fact, we need the Saviour.

Another important truth of this verse is that it takes any right away from me to criticize your way of living. If I criticize the things you do, then I am judging you for the same things I do. You might wonder if I do the same wrong things you do. Maybe not, but God says I do wrong, and wrong is wrong. I have all I can do to keep my relationship between me and Jesus in proper condition, without judging you.

The second verse is *Romans 6:23*. *"For the wages of sin is death, but the gift of God is eternal life through Jesus Christ our Lord."* Sometimes, we get all mixed up in terminology. You've heard of people becoming Christians, having eternal life, everlasting life, going to Heaven, being born again, being saved, and joining the Family of God. I have heard people say that they are one of the above, but not another, and so on.

But according to the scriptures, the terms all mean the same things. The term I like to use is that when I took the necessary steps by faith in Jesus, I joined the Family of God. This makes all Christians brothers and sisters in Christ.

In order to receive a gift, three facts have to be present. First, the gift has to be free. Second, the giver has to be willing to give it. And third, the recipient has to be willing to receive it. It cannot be a gift unless all of these facts are present.

If I told you I was going to give you a Bible, but I never did, it would never become a gift. If I charged you even ten cents for it, it would not be a gift because you paid for it. Therefore, it wasn't free.

On the other hand, I could be willing to give you this Bible free, and you could say, "Take your Bible, Eby, and keep it. I don't want it." It would never become a gift because you had exercised your right to reject it.

God has a free gift that He wants to give every one of us, but we have the right to accept it or reject it. If we don't accept it, then we reject it. Even though God wants all of us to have it, He will not force it on us, because He has given each of us a free choice.

You see, friends, we have a wonderful God. He has so set up His plan for our lives that no one has to go to Heaven if he doesn't want to. Isn't that wonderful? Because God gave Floyd Eby a choice, and I rejected it for many years, I should not force my beliefs on anyone else who isn't willing to read or listen. In fact, I always tell people that as I am talking to them about Jesus, if they don't want to hear it, just say so, and I will turn off. This is God's Way.

The third verse is *John 1:12*. *"But as many as received Him, to them gave He power to become the children of God, even to them that believe on His Name."* We have our choice, but if we do accept His gift, we immediately become a child of God.

I was brought up in a poor family on a farm in poverty conditions. What money we had, most of it had to go for my mother's doctor and hospital bills. I could not have the things that my friends had.

I couldn't even have a used bicycle, much less a car. I had to work when the other boys could play ball. I resented this poverty, and vowed I was going to do something about it.

You see, my mother and father loved me, but they were limited in what they could do for me because of the lack of material substance.

I sometimes wished that I had been born to a different Mom and Dad, so I could have the things some of my friends had. I realize now how foolish it was for my childish mind to think this way, but you see, my parents had limitations.

But when I joined the Family of God, God became my Heavenly Father, and He has no limitations like my earthly Mom and Dad had. My Heavenly Father owns the whole world and everything in it, and there is nothing that He cannot do.

He can give me health or He can let me lose it. He has done both in my lifetime. He can give me wealth or He can let me lose it. He has done both in my lifetime. He can keep my plane aloft, or let it crash. Praise God, He has done only one so far. It was and still is, a real thrill to join a family with a father with whom all things are possible.

The fourth verse is *Revelation 3:20*. *"Behold, I stand at the door, and knock, if any man hear my voice, and open the door, I will come in to him, and will sup with him, and he with me."* Since we know that God wrote the Bible, and that Jesus is God on the earth, then we know as we read the verse Revelation 3:20, it is actually Jesus speaking to you and me.

As I talk with people all over the United States, I find that great "hang-up" on Christianity is all the Do's and Don'ts that churches, ministers, and other Christians throw at people. But I find that God and His Word do not do this. There is absolutely nothing we have to do to acquire salvation. When Jesus spoke to me overseas He didn't say, "Floyd, I stand at the door and knock. If you quite cheating on your income tax, quit smoking, quit drinking, quit using drugs, quit swearing, quit running around on your wife, quit gambling, quit dancing, and hear my voice and invite me in, I will come in."

No, Jesus didn't put any conditions to my accepting Him as my Saviour and joining the Family of God, except to invite Him into my life, and believe and have faith that He will come in. All Jesus said was, "Floyd, I stand at the door and knock, and if you hear my voice and invite me in, I will come in, and you will become my child."

Jesus is no liar. He will do just that. Jesus is not talking about the front doors of our houses, but about our bodies. He says that He is ready at any time to send His Holy Spirit into our bodies and lives, and make us children of God, if we just invite Him in and mean it!

My Decision to Receive Christ As My Saviour

Confessing to God that I am a sinner, believing that the Lord Jesus died for my sins on the cross, and was raised for my justification, I do now receive and confess Him as my personal Saviour.

When I was overseas, in the United States Navy, at the age of 26, I took the three necessary steps, according to the Scriptures, and joined the Family of God.

To take *Step One:* I had to promise God that when He told me I am displeasing Him, I would come to Him, and be truly sorry and ask for His forgiveness, and He would forgive me. Please notice only God can tell me what I am doing wrong. He has the only right to judge me. You have no right because you are a sinner also.

Also, please notice that I do not have to tell any evangelist, minister, friend, relative, counselor, psychiatrist, or even my wife. I only have to tell Jesus, and He already knows, so that is no big deal, and did not present a problem to me. I sincerely promised Jesus that I would do this.

Step Two: I have to believe that Jesus, who is God upon the earth, died on the cross for your sins and my sins. Now, I don't understand this at all, but there is one part of it that I can understand. That is how Jesus can love you and me enough to give up His life for us, if that is the way He wants to do it.

I am sure if you have a son or daughter, and they were out in the street, and a huge truck was going to run over them, you would rush out to the street, and push them out of the way of the truck -- even though it meant losing your own life.

You would say, "Yes, I would do that because of my love for my children." However, I could offer you a million dollars to lay down in front of a large truck and be squashed to death, and you would turn the proposition down. You wouldn't sacrifice your life for money but you would for love. I would do the same for my daughters.

Now, if this is true of you and me, then we have to admit if we can love that much, then we know that Jesus, who is Divine, is capable of much greater love than you or I. So, certainly we can understand how He can love us enough to give up His life for us if that is the way He wants it.

I still don't understand how being nailed to the cross, crucified, and the shedding of His blood paid for my sins. But I don't have to understand, because He stated in the Bible that He wrote, that is the way He did it, and remember God is no liar!

Step Three: I have to believe that after Jesus was crucified and died on the cross, He was taken down and put in a tomb. Three days later He arose from the dead. Now, I don't understand how God did this, but I do know that God states four times in the Old Testament and four times in the New Testament in different words but all meaning the same thing: *that with God all things are possible -- and God is no liar!*

God wrote the Bible, and he said He arose from the dead, and so I believe it.

Salvation is *simple, sure, and complete.* We must promise

God that we will be truly sorry for our sins, we must believe that Jesus died on the cross for our sins, and that three days later Jesus arose from the dead for our justification. If we really mean it when we say to Jesus that we do believe, accept, and actually receive these three steps into our being as truth and by faith, then according to the scriptures, you and I are truly children of God and have joined the Family of God. We are truly brothers and sisters in Christ!

Congratulations on the greatest, most profitable, and wonderful decision you have ever made. God loves you and me, and I love you sister and brother!

"This poor man cried, and the
Lord heard him, and saved him
out of all his troubles."
Psalms 34:6

4

TURNING PROBLEMS INTO JOY

Since we now have joined the Family of God, what a wonderful, exciting, and tremendous adventure we have waiting for us.

God's Word is full of promises which He is anxiously waiting to fulfill for each one of His children. We now can expect to look forward to a life filled with exciting and wonderful events each and every day. We can look forward with anticipation to every new day, which can, and will be better than the day before.

I personally have been endowed with all of the secular things of this world we all seek -- even before I joined the Family of God. I was fortunate to have an excellent job in a wonderful profession, a wonderful family, much publicity, community status, a beautiful home, new cars, my own plane, many friends, successful businesses, money, state basketball championships, football and baseball championships, and many other honors during my short lifetime.

However, even though many of these accomplishments were exciting and thrilling, each one eventually became routine.

The new cars are great. But I didn't wash them much after the first month, and they soon faded into routine transportation.

The glow of athletic championships soon grew dim, and faded into just pleasant memories.

The making of money became an obsession that didn't leave time for the better things of life. The beautiful new home and swimming pool were wonderful, but soon became commonplace.

Becoming a successful business executive was a real boost to my ego, but presented many problems in living a happy, fruitful life. The publicity and honors made me feel important, but all were soon forgotten. When I first flew my own plane all by myself, I thought this was it. The ultimate. But it, too, became just a good way to travel.

All of the above became routine until I joined the Family of God, and I started using the above accomplishments to serve my Saviour. The only part of my life that never becomes routine is my personal relationship with the Lord Jesus. As I know Him better and better, every day gets better and better, and my relationship with Jesus is sweeter each and every day.

After we join the Family of God, Jesus only asks us to become His close friend. Another way of putting it is to grow spiritually, get closer to God, get to know Him better and better, putting God first, or increasing our faith. Jesus doesn't give us do's and don'ts. He just tells us how to become His close friend, and He will take care of everything else.

Each child of God is handled as a special case by Jesus. Our own relationship with Jesus has nothing to do with anybody else. He holds us responsible according to our spiritual age.

Let's say you are one year old, and you are walking. You

trip over your mom's best lamp and smash it. Your mother doesn't beat the tar out of you, because you are not old enough to know better. If you did it a few years later on purpose, she would let you know in no uncertain terms that it was wrong.

You see, friends, we hold our children responsible according to their chronological age, and the law also holds us reponsible to some degree according to our age. But God holds us responsible according to our spiritual age, and all of us may be at different spiritual ages or levels. How do I know this? Because there are things I could do a couple of years ago that were all right between me and my Saviour that I cannot do now, because I am now closer to God, and older spiritually.

Many times when dope addicts and alcoholics join the Family of God, the first question they ask is, "Do I have to give up my dope and alcohol now?"

I always reply, "You don't have to give up anything."

"What did you say?" They will ask.

"I said, you don't have to give up anything. Just make friends with Jesus. He will change your life at the accepted time, and you don't have to give up anything. He will take it away from you and make it a blessing.

"Each one of us is too weak to give up things, but God is strong. God will strengthen us through the Holy Spirit as we put Him first in our lives, and our lives will then change. I know it, because that is how God is changing my life."

After I became a Christian, I still played poker with my coaching friends. It was a small friendly game where you lose or win five or ten dollars during the evening. At the time it wasn't wrong between me and my Jesus to play poker, as He didn't speak to me about it.

However, as I grew spiritually, Jesus started speaking to me. He let me know that it wasn't a very good example to my coaching friends, and might instead be a stumbling block to their own personal encounter with Jesus.

I spoke back to the Lord, "Lord I love to play poker, and I

Accepted Jesus at an airport.

am not going to give it up."

As I continued to play each week, my leadings from the Lord became stronger. I finally rationalized that playing poker wasn't bad. It was winning that was bad. I decided I would continue to play poker, but I would make sure that I would not win. However, I didn't want to lose very much so I played it close to my belt, and tried to lose only a dollar or so.

I played three more weeks and I won each time. The only time I had ever been a consistent winner. I still refused to stop playing. I rationalized that playing poker wasn't bad, and winning wasn't bad, but taking the winnings home was bad. So when I would leave the game about midnight, I would take my winnings, put them in the next pot and tell my friends to play for them.

"Take your filthy earnings home, Eby. We don't want your filthy money. Take it, and forget it," they would remark sarcastically.

I would tell them I didn't want their money, and I would leave. After a couple of weeks of this, on my way home I thought, "here I am fighting God on this, and even making my best friends mad at me." That was the last of my poker playing.

TURNING PROBLEMS INTO JOY/69

You see, I really didn't give it up, but God took it away from me, and made it a real blessing. I no longer had God on my back, or my friends mad at me, and my wife was really happy. I felt good, and what a blessing it was to please Jesus. However, I am not saying it is wrong for other Christians if you gamble. It is wrong for a Christian to do anything that is displeasing to Jesus. He will let us know when we displease Him, and this will continually change as we grow spiritually.

The important question is how to grow spiritually -- how to know Him better and better -- how to get closer to God -- how to put God first -- how to increase our faith -- how to become a real close friend of Jesus?

When I first meet someone, I may decide that I really like this guy, and I want to become a real close friend of his. This would be impossible if I decided that I never want to see him again, never wrote to him, never telephoned him, or visited him. We would feel that such actions would be stupid, if we were really trying to be close friends.

On the same basis, we cannot become a close friend of Jesus if we refuse to read about Him in His Bible, refuse to talk to Him in prayer, refuse to be with His people, and refuse to serve Him.

To become a close friend of Jesus, or to grow spiritually, or to get to know Him better, or to be closer to God, or to put Him first, or to increase our faith, we need to follow Jesus' commands to 1. *Read the Bible*, 2. *Talk with God*, 3. *Be with other Christians*, 4. *Serve Jesus*.

Read the Bible

"Till I come, give attendance to reading"
1 Timothy 4:13a
"Study to show thyself approved unto God,
a workman that needeth not to be ashamed,
rightly dividing the word of truth."
2 Timothy 2:15

Many people after they have joined the Family of God (I have encouraged them to read the Bible) have come back and told me they were having trouble understanding it. I answer, "Hallelujah! Join the crowd. There are many things in the Bible I can't understand either. But God doesn't tell me that I must understand it; just that I must read or hear it."

If we do read or hear it, our Lord will reveal truths to us as we are ready for these truths, and He will bless our lives. However, if we refuse to read or hear it, He will not bless our lives by revealing truths from His Word. You and I could read the same chapter at the same time, and perhaps God would reveal a truth to you and not to me, because you are ready for that truth, and I am not yet ready.

The things in the Bible that I can't understand do not bother me. It is the things that I do understand that I have trouble with, and many truths in the Bible are very simple and easy to understand. I therefore have no excuse before Jesus when I displease Him by not following His guidelines for my life.

The real fundamental necessary truths needed for my salvation and spiritual growth were recorded in the Bible several times, in simple language, by several different Holy Men of God as they were directed by the Spirit of God.

Such fundamental beliefs as the Virgin Birth, the Crucifixion, The Resurrection, the Second Coming, and the belief that the Bible is God's Holy Inspired Word, are true and accurate because the original recordings were written by God Himself.

Controversial doctrine is important to us and to our numerous different denominations. I am sure it pleases God for us to join with other Christians in a local fellowship of like faith and doctrine to promote the cause of Jesus.

However, I believe there are only two groups when it comes to spirituality. Either we are believers or unbelievers. And if we are not believers, we are unbelievers. It is important that we love the Lord Jesus Christ, and accept in faith the fundamental truths necessary to join the Family of God according to the Scriptures.

I believe much misunderstanding comes from the term "church" in the Bible. When God uses the term "church" in His Bible, I believe He is referring to a group of believers gathering for the purpose of worshipping our Lord. This can include all of the different denominations, organizations, church buildings, missionary groups, broadcasting, television, home Bible studies, prayer meetings, meetings in cars, planes, or on the job. I don't believe our Lord would just have us equate the biblical term church with a denominational organization and a church building.

We need to read the Bible daily, and the more we read, the more our Jesus will bless us with the truths needed to live a happy, fruitful life.

Talk With God

In the Bible, God commands us to talk or pray to Him. *1 Timothy 2:8 "I will, therefore, that men pray everywhere, lifting up holy hands, without wrath and doubting."*

1 Thessolonians 5:17 "Pray without ceasing." *Acts 6:4 "But we will give ourselves continually to prayer, and to the ministry of the Word."* *Luke 18:1 "And He spoke a parable unto them to this end, that men ought always to pray, and not to faint."*

To become a close friend to anyone, we need to talk and visit with them. The same is true if we become a close friend to Jesus; we need to talk and visit with Him, which many call prayer. We can talk to Him in public or in private, on our knees, or in any position, out loud or without utterance, at any time, and at any place, and about any thing. To grow spiritually, we need to talk to God many times a day, and He will bless us for it!

Let us not forget to praise Him and pray for others as well as ourselves.

Be With Other Christians

The Bible commands us to join in fellowship with believers, and people of like faith. *Acts 2:42 "And they continued steadfastly in the apostles' doctrine and fellowship, and in breaking of bread, and in prayers." I John 1:3 "That which we have seen and heard declare we unto you, that ye also may have fellowship with us; and truly our fellowship is with the Father, and with His Son, Jesus Christ." I John 1:7 "But if we walk in the light, as He is in the light, we have fellowship one with another, and the blood of Jesus Christ, His Son cleanseth us from all sin."*

You would probably like to ask me if I ever associate with unbelievers? I certainly do. I have hundreds of coaching friends who believe just as I do. I also have hundreds of friends who do not believe as I do. I have spent many a night talking basketball and football with coaching friends who were not Christians.

I enjoyed these evenings very much, and there is not anything wrong with it. However, I have to admit that when I am with my unbelieving friends, nothing happens to get me closer to the Lord. In fact, I am drawn away from God. So you see, I need to spend the majority of my time with other people of like faith if I want to become a closer friend of Jesus, grow spiritually, get to know Him better, and better, or increase my faith.

Christian people surrounding us with their presence, their compassion, concern, and love, will have a real influence on our spiritual growth. We have to be real strong spiritually, to keep an environment of unbelievers from dragging us away from our God.

What are some of the ways to obtain the needed Christian fellowship? Following is a suggested list: churches and other Christian Service organizations, Christian friends, home Bible studies, Christian meetings, retreats, and conferences, your own program of serving Jesus, Christian Schools, Christian parties, Christian excursions, the making of your own home into a place of Christian gatherings.

Serve Jesus

We are commanded by the Bible to obey and serve Jesus. *John 12:26 "If any man serve me, let him follow me; and where I am, there shall also my servant be; if any man serve me, him will my Father honour." Colossians 3:23, 24 "And whatsoever ye do, do it heartily, as to the Lord, and not unto men." "Knowing that of the Lord ye shall receive the reward of the inheritance; for ye serve the Lord Christ." Ephesians 6:7 "With good will doing service, as to the Lord, and not to men."*

When we start serving Jesus through His leading, we will really grow rapidly spiritually and get close to God. As we serve Him regularly, we will become His best friend, and He will shower us with abundant blessings. I don't know how God will have you serve Him, but I do know that if we grow spiritually, He will tell us how He would have us serve Him.

I am sure God would have you serve Him differently than He has me. All I can do is tell you what doors of service He has opened for me: Giving messages about the Bible and My Lord at banquets, churches, schools, clubs, conferences and conventions; a witnessing and personal follow-up program; my church and many other service organizations; home Bible studies, television programs, jail ministry; counseling couples with marital trouble; counseling alcoholics, dope addicts, and law violators concerning help from God and the Bible; writing Christian books, and through other avenues of service.

God has opened so many doors that now it is thrilling to watch how He can guide me into new service by closing doors in present service. I can sincerely say that I have never been any happier than I am now when He has opened so many doors through which I can walk and receive real blessings. Praise His Holy Name!

Family Devotions

74/MIRACLES OF LOVE

God will bless any family of believers who will designate a time each day and have a devotional period with all members of the family present. When you have it, during the day or night, will depend on the time necessary to have everyone present. Our devotional period is in the morning before breakfast, and consists of the reading of a portion of God's Word, an illustration about the reading, prayer requests, and prayer.

A church goer for many years now coming to know Jesus personally.

We know that forty per cent of all marriages today end up in divorce. But recent surveys taken of thousands of families who are Christians, go to church and other Christian meetings together, have daily devotions, read the Bible together daily, pray together daily, and take their problems to the Lord, indicate that only one out of 900 such marriages end up in divorce. I am sure you will agree that there is no marriage counselor, psychologist, psychiatrist, minister, or anyone else who can bring about such results. But God's precious Holy Inspired Word, the Bible, and the Holy Spirit can.

Things

Through my many years of working with all kinds of people with problems, I have found only one solution: The

TURNING PROBLEMS INTO JOY/75

Bible and God. I have also found that 90 per cent of the people have "hang-ups" on Christianity, preachers, churches, Christians, and the Bible, because of all of the do's and don'ts that all the Christians have thrown at them. They have been told they would have to do this and not be able to do that. You must not smoke, drink, use dope, dance, play cards, wear mini-skirts, commit adultery, swear, steal, etc. I call this a list of "things."

I sincerely believe that no minister ever changed a person's life by preaching "things" from the pulpit. God's Word put no restrictions or do's and don'ts in joining the Family of God. We need to preach and teach Jesus Christ and His Word in every temple and every house.

As a person joins the Family of God and then grows spiritually under the preaching and teaching of Jesus Christ, then that person will have his life changed by the removal of the "things" by God at the accepted time.

Home Bible Studies

Acts 5:42 "And daily in the temple, and in every house, they ceased not to teach and preach Jesus Christ." I believe that we have attempted to spread the News of a Wonderful Saviour in the wrong way. We have established beautiful church buildings, hired articulate preachers, trained Sunday School teachers, organized our churches and Sunday schools to the utmost, purchased buses, and had evangelistic meetings.

We have then waited for the unsaved to come in, or have contests to draw them in or have calling programs to try and get them to the church. I am not saying that the above methods are wrong, but we have to admit the methods listed have not produced enough of the desired results.

Jesus traveled to where people were. He did not stay in one place and wait for people to show up. Jesus said, "Go, Ye." I believe we have to follow the example of Jesus; we need to go to where people are. We need to go into homes;

not to invite them to church, but to tell them about Jesus. We can "beat" a person over the head enough, and get him to church even two Sundays in a row. Then he stays home the third Sunday, and we have to start all over again.

Why should an unsaved person enjoy coming to church or to evangelistic meetings? Did you, before you were saved? We need to visit people in their own surroundings and explain salvation to them. Once they have joined the Family of God, and start growing in the Word, most of them will then want to come to church to be fed in the Word by our ministers, have fellowship with God's Children, and want to serve Jesus.

We need to go to the homes, hippie communes, jails, hospitals, sanitariums, schools, civic clubs, and any other place that God opens up, and talk to people about Jesus and the Bible. We need to talk to people we work with, on breaks and at noon hours. We need to talk to them on the street, or during recreation whenever God opens a door.

People who will never attend a church will allow you to come to their home, if approached properly under God's Guidance, to talk with them about the Bible and Jesus and this new way of life. Neighbors will also come to your own home to read and discuss the Bible if you invite them. The home Bible study should be voluntary and permit free will in every aspect.

Don't "bug" people if they miss; just keep inviting them. Be available, and pray for them, and let them know that you are praying for them. No one reads unless they choose to. Don't ask questions of specific individuals unless you are sure they are willing. Just throw the question out to the group. Let them comment or give illustrations if they desire.

Don't put anyone on the spot. Be simple in your teaching. Give them milk until they are ready for the meat. Teach the fundamental necessities of joining the Family of God and of growing spiritually. Don't argue controversial doctrine. Emphasize the importance of loving the Lord Jesus, and do not push your own convictions down other people's throats.

God gave each one of us a choice, and we have no right to insist that others agree with us. The length of the Bible study will depend on the people involved, conditions, and God's leading.

However, none of them should "drag". In one home I only spend from five to ten minutes, reading a few verses of scripture, make a few comments, ask for their prayer requests, and close in prayer. On the other hand, I have a home Bible study that lasts 90 minutes. Between these two extremes are many others with varying times.

Every new person should, within a few weeks, if not the same night, be taken through the scriptures, have God's Plan for his or her life explained, and be given the opportunity to make a decision. Of course this is dependent on their desire to do so.

Be sure to make friends first. Don't talk "things" or problems; just talk Jesus and how to join His Family; how to get close to Him. Encourage people to get close to Him by reading the Bible, talking with Jesus, being with other Christians, and serving Jesus. All other "things" are up to God.

Discipline

We must discipline ourselves to grow spiritually and get close to God. It takes discipline on our part to do the things necessary to come close to God. It takes discipline to read the Bible daily, to pray daily, to be with Christians, and to serve Jesus.

Many times there is other literature I would rather read than the Bible, but I know that the Bible only can give me a happy, fruitful life. So I must set a time aside daily to read the Bible even if I would rather not.

It takes discipline to pray daily especially when everything is going well. It is easy to spend time in prayer when we have problems like illness that we cannot handle. But how much time do we spend talking to God when we don't have problems? God said, "Pray without ceasing."

It takes discipline to be with other Christians. It might seem to be more fun to skip that Christian meeting and go to the ball game or go bowling, but our real happiness depends on fellowship of Christians to give us strength, and assurance for a really happy way of life.

It takes discipline to serve Jesus when He calls us or leads us to serve Him. Sometimes, I would rather sit at home than to make a needed call. I am tired and weary, but fatigue is mainly of the mind, and the joy of serving Jesus will completely rest us.

When we are completely exhausted over a period of time, God is able and will give us time to recover. Many times I have reached this point, and God has downed me and my plane with bad weather for a day or two. I come back home completely rested. Our Wonderful Saviour knows and understands all of our needs.

Commitment

How can we have all our prayers answered? How can we have all the bad things that happen to us turn out good? How can we have all of God's promises fulfilled in our lives? I sincerely believe that all of the above can be fulfilled in all of the believers' lives.

It can happen to each of us as we simply covenant with our Lord Jesus to make and keep a deep commitment to continually strive to put God first in our lives at all times!

I am married to a wonderful woman named Betty. This marriage has lasted over 38 years. If I put four other women ahead of my wife in our marriage, it will not be a satisfactory marriage relationship. In fact if you know my Betty, if I put one woman ahead of her, it will not be a good marriage.

The only way I can have a satisfactory marriage relationship with my wife is by putting her the top woman in my life, and for her to put me the top man in her life. At the present time that is what both of us are doing and we have a wonderful marriage relationship

But what about our relationship with God? Can we put four other things in our lives ahead of our God, or twenty, or fifty, or even one, and have a successful relationship with Him? I believe the answer is simple. If my wife won't tolerate anything but being first in my life, my God won't either! Therefore, if I want a blessed, happy, fruitful life, I need to put my God first!

I am sure you readers are thinking, "Coach, do you always put God first in your life?" I have to admit to you that I don't. I am also weak. But I can honestly tell you that when I do, great things happen in my life, and when I don't, things get sticky and messy.

I would like to point out to you three verses of scriptures. *Psalm 37:5 "Commit thy way unto the Lord; trust also in Him; and he shall bring it to pass."* What is God really saying to me? I believe He is telling me, "Coach, live a life pleasing to me and put me first in your life, then take every problem you have, health, family problems, finances, jobs, etc. and place them all into my hands and forget them as I will take care of them!" God said that. God is no liar, and if I put Him first in my life He will take care of everything.

Romans 8:28 "And we know that all things work together for good to them that love God, to them who are the called according to His purpose." I know that according to Revelation I am not to add or subtract from the scriptures, but for my own use I paraphrase the above verse: All things work out to good for those who love God, if I love Him enough to put Him first in my life. Then it works for me.

Revelation 21:4 "And God shall wipe away all tears from their eyes; and there shall be no more death, neither sorrow, nor crying, neither shall there be any more pain; for the former things are passed away." In this verse, God has indicated that He has the right to use us believers any way that He desires while we are upon this earth, because He has guaranteed our future for eternity!

If I told you that if you would work for me just one hour in a terrible job, but it wouldn't kill you and it wasn't dishonest, I would promise you all the money you could spend during the rest of your life time on this earth, I am sure you would say, "Lead me to that job Coach, I can stand anything for one hour to insure my entire future financially."

Friends that is what God is telling us, "Children, if you will just let me use your lives while on this earth any way I want to, and to my Glory, I will insure your future for eternity, forever and forever."

Do we realize that one hour compared to a life time of even seventy years is much, much more than seventy years compared to eternity! Please God help me to praise and thank you no matter what happens to me on this earth, because you have promised me the future for forever with no problems!

How Christians Can Help Others

Nearly all people need help, believers and unbelievers alike. As Christians we need to help people. We need to be willing under God's Guidance to spend our time, material substance, and talent. However, I am convinced that though we need to be concerned about peoples' physical needs, we never really are of any real help unless we include the spiritual needs.

In my humble opinion, there are three things that we believers can do for unbelievers, and back sliding believers. The first is to pray for them even when we don't want to. Second, we need to get as close to God as we possibly can ourselves. Remember, people are watching us and will see how God is changing our life. This can have more influence on others than anything else. Thirdly, don't ever "bug" other people, just love them! Criticism turns people off, but they cannot resist or fight the love of Jesus.

As I counsel with people who are children of God, I suggest they go on a spiritual program for 60 days, and then evaluate the results. The spiritual program I suggest is as follows:

1. Daily Bible reading.
2. Frequent communication with God each day.
3. Daily devotionals with the family or by themselves.
4. Consistent attendance at a church of their choice.
5. A weekly Bible study with friends.
6. Consistent fellowship with other Christians.
7. Serve our Lord Jesus as He directs.

I have yet to know a believer who sincerely followed the above program without finding the power of God's life in solving their problems. On the other hand, we believers who do not follow God's program for our life will not receive help from Him!

When a prison inmate professes Jesus, I encourage him to come to me as soon as he is released from jail. I will then give him the above spiritual program. I notify him that if he follows the spiritual program consistently that God will guarantee that he will never go back to jail. And if he doesn't follow it, I will guarantee that he will go back to jail. That is the way it works out.

For example, when I find Charlie back in jail, I say to him: "Congratulations Charlie."

"What for?" he will ask.

"For being back in jail," I reply.

"Are you crazy, Coach? I didn't want to come back to jail," he will protest.

"Yes you did," I will insist. "You asked God to put you back in jail and He gave you your wish."

"What makes you say that Coach?"

"Well Charlie, how long did you stay on that spiritual program?"

"Two weeks," he replied.

"When did you come back to jail Charlie?"

"The third week," he admits.

"You see Charlie, you asked God to put you back into jail when you quit following His Spiritual Program for your life, and He granted your request."

However, friend, the prison inmate is no different than you and me as believers. When we go off of God's Spiritual Program for our lives, we are asking for problems that will mess up our lives, and we are granted our request.

I personally have compassion for all believers who are helpless physically, mentally, and emotionally. I will spend time to help them in any way I can. However, this is a very small group, as most people can help themselves in some way.

I also have compassion for those believers who can help themselves and are trying to do so. I will spend all the time that my Lord will make possible to help them.

The largest group of believers is made up of people who can help themselves, but will not make an effort to do so. I still love this group and will continue to pray for them.

But I will not waste the Lord's time trying to help believers who will not attempt to go on the spiritual program, or make a sincere effort to consistently follow it. I am wasting my time and the Lord's time if I try to help people who will not lift a finger to help themselves to follow God's Program for their lives.

Remember, believer, the devil can give us fun, but only God can give us joy. Fun is only temporary, but joy is lasting. Don't seek fun from the devil that creates so many problems for us, but seek joy from Jesus which will solve our problems.

Believer, don't be discouraged when God doesn't take all our bad habits from us. I sincerely believe that each one of us will have a "thorn" with which we will always have to battle. The Apostle Paul did, and God never took it away from him.

If our Lord took everything away from us, we would not need Him any more. We are always going to be dependent on God. Believers, don't criticize other people's "thorns." Perhaps their "thorn" shows and ours doesn't, but God sees all "thorns."

*"Be not deceived; God is not mocked:
for whatsoever a man soweth, that
shall he also reap."*
Galatians 6:7

5

CHRISTIANITY DOESN'T ALWAYS WORK

Isn't That Asking Too Much?

"Isn't that asking too much, Coach?" Clara asked. "You have me going to church three times each Sunday. I think that's just too much."

"It is all in the way you look at it, Clara," I replied. "How many times a day would you be willing to go to a tavern? A dozen?"

"At least two dozen times," she quickly replied.

"There we are, Clara. We are willing to do the things we want to do as many times as we want, but when it comes to pleasing God, we want to limit Him."

Clara had professed Jesus two years before, but she would not stay on the spiritual program. She split with her husband and they both went in different directions. I lost track of Clara for a year. She had once again hit the dope, alcoholic, and prostitution trail.

Some men had beaten her after misusing her. She was taken to the hospital, and after three days of recovery, she called me.

"Coach Eby, this is Clara, and I need to see you. Will you please come? I need to get right with God."

I flew to the city and took a taxi to the hospital. As I walked down the corridor I saw her sitting in a chair in the hall. There she was, formerly an attractive lady. She was 36, but looked like she was 80. Living a life displeasing to Jesus had really taken its toll.

She took me into her room, threw her arms around me and kissed me.

"Coach, I got to get right with God. Please, please help me get right with God. I just have to get right with God. Please help me."

"Clara, you were right with God at one time. Remember how you decided you were going to limit God as to how much you were going to try and please Him? It just doesn't work that way, Clara. We have to continually strive to please Him, if we are going to live a blessed and fruitful life."

"Just get me out of this hospital, and give me another chance. I will do anything you ask to me to do - anything," she promised!

"I don't want you to do what I want you to do, Clara. Just do what God wants you to do."

"I will do everything He wants me to do," she answered.

After four days of making arrangements with the hospital, therapists, and psychiatrists, I was able to bring Clara back home.

One of the couples in my home Bible studies took her into their home, and showed her the love and attention she needed. Within one week God had already blessed her as she followed His spiritual program. God is good. Clara now looked 36 years old again; she had her own apartment, and had a job.

Fox six weeks, Clara followed the program. She had decided to go to only Sunday School on Sunday. Of course this soon resulted in not going at all.

In a few days Clara had left the program entirely. Soon after I was called to go down to a local tavern to pull her out. She was sousing drunk. Three days later she was picked up by the police as she laid unconscious in her parked car.

The judge sentenced Clara to ninety days in the local jail. He would not listen to her many promises.

I visited her several times while she was in jail. She had a lot of time on her hands, and spent much of it reading the Bible and writing letters. When she was discharged, she was once again close to the Lord. After a session of prayer and discussion with me, Clara traveled to Florida.

The first couple of letters were encouraging, but soon afterwards a phone call indicated to me that the devil had once again pulled her away from God's Program. I will never quit praying for my friend, Clara, or stop loving her. But I cannot help her stay on God's spiritual program unless she is willing to please Jesus herself.

Christianity only works when we are continually willing and striving to live a life pleasing to Him!

Religion and I Don't Mix

As I was holding meetings in an adjacent state, I met the Christian parents of a nineteen year old son, just one year out of high school. Daryl J. is a likable fellow, but he wanted nothing to do with spiritual things.

I made friends with Daryl, who is a "nut" on pro basketball. His favorite team is the Philadelphia Sixers, and his favorite player is Julius Erving who has been nicknamed "Dr. J." Upon meeting Daryl J. and finding out about his love for pro basketball, I immediately nicknamed Daryl, "Dr. J" and he loved it. We became such good friends that Daryl even came to a church to hear me speak.

After returning home, I received a letter from Daryl. He thanked me for showing him that religion didn't need to be "stuffy." But he really wasn't interested.

However, Daryl informed me that he had a problem and he thought I could help him.

"Coach, although I am nineteen I am in love with a fifteen year old girl, and she is in love with me. Now Coach this is not 'puppy' love. This is the real thing. We really love each other and want to get married, but her Dad doesn't think much of it, and won't even let me see her. Coach, here is my girl friend's father's name, address, and telephone number. Would you please write to him and also call him and convince him that I am a strictly Number One guy?"

I wrote back to Daryl. "Dear Dr. J: I am sorry that I cannot be of any help with your prospective father-in-law. But I can tell you about Jesus who can help you with any and all of your problems."

I went on to describe how Daryl could become a member of the Family of God, and I also told him how he could turn his life over to Jesus, and let Him handle his problems.

I received the following letter from Daryl. "Coach, my girlfriend's name is Brenda. She already has one of your books. She received it the day you spoke at the high school.

"Look Coach, God and I haven't made it in five previous tries, so I don't bother with him any more. Religion and I don't mix. God offers one thing by being a Christian, eternal life. Myself, I don't care about that. I am out to help others through love, caring, understanding, humor and kindness. No snow jobs, Coach. My mind is blocked out when it comes to religion. Mom and Dad crammed it down my throat and turned me against it. They never gave me the chance to accept it on my own. They meant well, but they blew it! Reading your book won't phase me. Thanks anyway, I appreciate your kindness. Christ wouldn't solve things with my girlfriend's father instantly, it would take time. I am willing to be patient and let time take its course without God. Except for swearing, I lead a life quite pleasing to Jesus, but things aren't any better anyway. Tons of people and parents know that I am an all right guy. Brenda's father won't give me a chance to prove why. People have told me that if the world was like me, it would be great. Christ has had nothing to do with it. Sincerely Yours, Daryl J."

I wrote back. "Dear Dr. J. This will be the last time that I will ever mention the Bible and Jesus to you, unless you ask me to. You see, Daryl, you have the right to choose, and I will not force my convictions on you. However, Dr. J., as a real friends of yours, I must say one more thing.

"Dr. J., you will never make it in this world without Jesus. You will never have a happy, fruitful, wonderful life without turning your life over to Him. I am sorry, but that is the way it is. I pray that you and I can still be friends."

Praise God for answered prayers. Several weeks later I received the the following letter from "Dr. J."

"Dear Coach Eby, could you write Brenda? We are in love and we do want to spend the rest of our lives together. It looks like Heaven is the only place we can. Plus I can't find a job. I need extra help. God's help. Could you talk to Brenda about her and I turning our lives over to Christ?

"On the level, I need Him. We both do. Please tell Brenda how it could make things better with our parents, friends and ourselves. Sincerely Yours, Daryl J."

I am now corresponding with both "Dr. J." and Brenda. I believe that both of them will soon accept Jesus. They will then be in a position to receive help from Him!

I Am Mixed Up

"Coach, I would like to have you talk to my daughter," a lady requested. She is only sixteen, a senior in high school, and she is pregnant."

"I will on one condition," I answered. "That she wants to talk to me."

"I want her to talk with you and she will, I will see to that," Ruth replied.

"That is not good enough," I stated. "You know where I live and she can call me or come to see me if she personally cares to," I said.

A week later Jean came to me. I had never met her. I told her about Jesus, and she professed Him. I started taking Jean with me to a midnight Bible Study. She entered into the discussions and also took a turn in praying.

She started growing spiritually, but one night as I was taking her home from Bible Study she started a discussion.

"Coach, I do love Jesus, and it seems so great that I can call on Him at any time for help. However, I am mixed up."

Of course, Jean was mixed up. She was getting all kinds of advice from her friends. I knew without asking her what she was being advised.

From jail to the Kingdom of God.

"Don't marry the bum."

"Marry him and give your child a name."

"Don't marry him but give your baby up for adoption so it will have a chance."

"Don't give up your baby. Keep it or you will always be sorry."

"Don't do any of these, just have an abortion and forget it."

Why wouldn't Jean be mixed up with all of her friends giving her all different kinds of advice?

"Coach, I trust you and I want to know what you think I should do," she said.

"Sure, Jean, I can tell you what you should do. Keep getting as close to God as you possibly can, and listen and He will tell you what to do. Jean, we humans make mistakes but our Lord never does." Jean kept her beautiful baby, and she is now married.

God's Accepted Time

As I was having meetings in Houston, Texas, a couple from my home state of Michigan came to see me.

"Coach, we have our eighteen year old daughter with us. We wish you would talk to her. Dolly is very rebellious. She is anti-church and anti-Jesus. She is living a very messy life."

I agreed to talk to my friends' daughter if Dolly was willing. Later, when I saw Dolly and introduced myself, I was unable to make friends with her. She let me know that she wasn't really interested in the new way of life I wanted to talk to her about.

I excused myself and left. I did not see her for more than a year, but I kept her picture on my prayer board and I prayed for her regularly. I wrote to her but she didn't answer. I called her, but she refused to talk with me.

Whenever I met friends who knew Dolly I would ask how she was. Each time, the report was worse. I quit asking. I just knew that I wasn't God's servant to talk to Dolly, or it wasn't His accepted time. I no longer attempted to make contact as I sincerely believed that God had definitely closed the door as far as I was personally concerned.

About three years after the Houston confrontation with Dolly, I was speaking at a meeting about 100 miles from my home. I happened to sit next to Dolly's parents whom I didn't recognize. They introduced themselves to me, and even though I didn't want to, I had to ask how Dolly was.

"Coach, for the first time in a long time Dolly is now home with us with her baby. Her ex-husband is in jail. Would you give her a telephone call?"

I dialed the number and Dolly answered.

"Is this Dolly?" I asked.

"Who is this?" she asked suspiciously.

"Do you remember me Dolly? I am that big monster who met you in Houston, Texas, three years ago. Coach Eby."

"Sure, I remember you! Would you come over to visit me tonight?"

I assured her I would be over as soon as the meeting ended. Dolly's parents were going to take me to the airport. I went to their house with them.

After greeting Dolly and meeting her beautiful baby, I asked if she would like to talk with me alone. She said she would, so her parents took the baby and went into another room, while Dolly and I remained in the kitchen.

As I started telling Dolly about God's Plan for her life, she interrupted.

"Coach, I am not ready to accept Jesus as yet. There are too many things I need to change in my life first."

"Dolly," I said, "That's going at it the wrong way. After we accept Jesus, He will change our lives and make it a blessing."

Dolly professed Jesus that night and joined the Family of God. Later, she wrote to me. "Coach, I am not interested in my ex-husband as a husband, but I am interested in his soul. Would you please send him one of your books, and a Bible, and write to him?"

A few days later I received a very sarcastic and curt letter from Dolly's ex-husband, Pete.

"Sir, I wish to thank you for the free book that you wrote, but I want you to know that I will not read it. I am not interested in that stuff."

A week later I received another letter from Pete.

"Sir, I left your book lying around for three days. I then picked it up and started reading it. It became fascinating. After the cell lights were shut off, I stood up on my bunk. I could continue reading as the outside lights came shining through the barred window. Sir, I need to talk with you about this Jesus."

Three days later I flew my airplane up to the prison to visit three inmates. One of them was Pete. As I sat down alone

CHRISTIANITY DOESN'T ALWAYS WORK/91

with Pete in the prison yard, I told him about the salvation Jesus had for him. Pete professed Jesus and joined the Family of God. He studied the Bible, attended chapel services, and completed correspondence Bible Courses.

However, I have not been in touch with Dolly for some time, and reports indicate that she is in trouble again spiritually. She has fallen away from God's spiritual program for her life.

All of us can be like Dolly. If we do not discipline ourselves to keep close to God, we will not be blessed by our Lord. We will have troubles and a messy life. Christianity does not work unless we put God first in our lives.

Marriages Kept Me From God

Barb, who had professed Jesus, was telling me about her past and present problems concerning her ex-husbands.

"I was real close to God when I first married. I was reading the Bible daily, fellowshipping with other Christians, and felt a real personal relationship with Jesus. After marriage, my husband didn't want to go to church or read the Bible with me. He would always drag his feet on anything spiritual. I decided not to offend him and go along with his way of living. Our marriage deteriorated rapidly. Our problems became greater, and our marriage was no longer worth it, and we ended up in divorce.

"Once again, living by myself, I got back with God. I read the Bible regularly, communicated with Him, and went to church and Bible Study regularly. A couple of years later, I married once again. This husband also wasn't interested in spiritual things. I quit going to church and Bible Study. I started limiting my Bible reading and devotionals. My second marriage also ended up in divorce.

"Coach, I love Jesus, and I know I am a child of God. Why doesn't Jesus bless my life and marriages?"

"Barb," I answered, "You know what you are telling me? You are telling me that your husbands and your marriages pulled you away from God. Do you think that our Lord is going to bless anything that pulls us away from Him? No way! God only blesses us when we put Him first in our life. Not when we put Him last!" Barb found the answer. Being within the Will of God is much more important than being married.

Playing Games With God

"Coach, you say you love me, but you won't lift a finger to help me when I need help. You claim to be a Christian, but refuse to help me. Just forget the whole thing," he said, and he hung up.

Dick had just phoned me to ask me to co-sign a note so he could buy a car.

Dick had professed Jesus several years before, but ever since then he had been playing games with God. A very likable guy, he was a real con man. He was most convincing. He could con almost anyone into anything. But Dick apparently forgot that in no way could he or anyone con God.

God gave Dick some talent in singing, playing the guitar, and in composing songs. And for some time he followed a spiritual program for his life --- playing and singing for church and Bible Study, driving the church's bus for Sunday School, attending church and Bible studies. He had been happier than ever before. He had a good relationship with his girl friend.

But Dick left God's Program, and his life deteriorated rapidly. Several Christians helped him get jobs that he didn't keep. He borrowed money that he didn't pay back. He took advantage of anyone he could, including his mother.

He was living a life completely displeasing to his God, at the time of his phone call. He had lost his girl friend, and he lived a life of running around and sponging off of other people.

I do love Dick and I pray for him regularly. However, I

From hippies to God's chosen.

will not help him again materially until I know he is no longer playing games with God. Not because I am sour about the past, but because I believe helping him materially now is really hurting him.

I don't believe that he will lean and depend upon God until we humans quit paying for his mistakes. I pray I will soon see the day that Dick will completely turn his life over to Jesus. Until he quits playing games with God, he will not have the wonderful, happy, fruitful life that only Jesus can give.

We Are Weak But God Is Strong

Jake professed the Lord in the county jail, and Jill accepted the Lord at a church crusade. While Jake was spending time in Jackson prison, I married him and Jill in a Christian ceremony in a special cell.

Their professions to being children of God seemed real. While he was serving out the remainder of his term, Jake seemed to become closer and closer to God. He was spending a lot of time in Bible Study, and started some Bible Studies among his fellow inmates.

On the outside, Jill was attending Church and a weekly

Bible Study with her son. God was blessing them even though they were apart except for routine visits at the prison.

Upon Jake's discharge from Jackson prison, it appeared that the three were in a position to be blessed by God as a Christian Family. They rented a mobile home and Jake secured a job. As a Christian family the three attended church and a weekly Bible Study regularly.

A few months later, worshipping together became very irregular. Jill started playing softball on Wednesday nights which conflicted with the weekly Bible study.

Jake kept attending but not as regularly as before. Family church attendance became irregular. This was a sure sign of problems.

Jill left God's spiritual program completely and started living a life displeasing to her Jesus. Jake also started slipping and breaking probation. Because of a probation violation, Jake was sent back to Jackson prison, and divorce proceedings were started.

As I attended Jake's parole board hearing, I met Jill again for the first time in a long while. She came to me after the hearing, wanting to know why all of this had happened. Why did God let it happen?

"Jill," I answered, "You are not responsible for Jake, but you are responsible for keeping your own relationship right with Jesus. Jake is responsible for keeping his relationship right with Jesus."

"I've tried, I've tried," she whimpered, "But it just doesn't seem to work out."

"Come on, Jill, you know better than that," I interrupted. "When were you the happiest? Back when you were following God's program or now?"

She acknowledged that she wasn't happy now.

"You see, Jill, you and Jake are going to have to learn what all Christians have to learn. It is all or nothing with our Lord. We can't play games with Him. We need to put Him first in our life to live a happy, fruitful life. Let's go all out with God!"

CHRISTIANITY DOESN'T ALWAYS WORK/95

My prayer for both Jake and Jill is that they will completely surrender their lives to a loving and living God who will guide their lives and will eliminate their mistakes!

Don't You Know?

I was making some door-to-door calls as part of a three-day crusade at a church. I had been given referrals by people from the church. On this particular day, the local Pastor was with me. As I knocked on the door I wasn't certain that I was at the right house. I had been referred to a lady by the name of Charlene who had two children but was living alone.

A man opened the door. "Does Charlene live here?" I asked.

"Yes," he answered, "I am her husband. What do you want?"

"I am Coach Eby, and I am having meetings at a local church," I explained.

"I am doing some calling, telling people about a new way of life. This new way of life is tremendous. It is free and will work miracles in our lives and will take over all of our problems. Wouldn't you like to hear about it?"

"I don't much go for that religious stuff," he replied.

"What do you have to lose?" I offered. "You can turn me off any time you wish, and I will leave. Isn't that fair enough?"

"Well, come on in," Del said uncertainly. "I might listen for a few minutes."

"What about letting me invite my Preacher friend in? He is out in the car."

"No, I don't want a preacher in here," Del protested.

"Oh come on, Del, my preacher friend is an all right guy. I will personally vouch for him. Let him come in with me."

"Well, OK," Del reluctantly agreed.

As Del showed us into the kitchen, Charlene was leaning against the kitchen cabinets, dressed in an extremely short skirt. I went over to her and shook her hand and introduced myself. Del asked us to sit down at the table in the dining area.

"Why don't you come over and sit down with us, Charlene, where you can hear better?" I asked.

"Nope," she answered. Charlene remained leaning against the kitchen cabinets. I started talking to both of them about the Bible and Jesus.

Del interrupted. "I bet you know all about me, don't you?"

"Not at all," I replied. "I never met you before in my life, and I don't know one thing about you."

"You're telling me that you didn't know that I just got out of Jackson Prison two weeks ago today?" Del asked.

"No, I didn't know," I answered. "What difference does that make? I just got out of Jackson prison myself three weeks ago last Sunday."

Both of Del's and Charlene's eyes opened wide. They gazed at me in astonishment.

"Is that really true?" Charlene blurted out.

"Yes it is," I answered. "However, I was speaking at Chapel Services." They both seemed to be more attentive after that.

I talked to Del and Charlene for about twenty minutes. I asked them if the points I was making didn't make sense. They were reluctant to agree, but they refused to turn me off even when I asked them if they wanted to.

Then Charlene excused herself and left the room. In a few minutes she came back and had changed clothes from the very short skirt into slacks. She still didn't sit down with us but leaned against the cabinets. I do believe God had been speaking to her.

I completed the presentation of God's plan for each one of their lives. Del and Charlene were reluctant to make a commitment.

"It's been great, Del and Charlene, to meet you and your children, and talk with you about the Bible and Jesus. Would you mind giving me your address so I can write to you? Also, could we close our time together with a circle prayer?"

Del and Charlene both agreed. The four of us held hands in a circle. I asked the Pastor to ask Our Lord's Blessing upon our new found friends. I knew the seed had been sewn.

After arriving home I wrote to Del and Charlene, but I didn't hear from them. Three months later, on the way to another meeting, I flew into the area airport to give some of the kids a free airplane ride.

Del and Charlene were there with their two children. They were glad to see me. I now knew they were my friends.

As I taxied down the runway with Del in front with me, and Charlene in the back seat with the two children, I turned to the back seat and spoke to Charlene.

"When I first met you, Charlene, you were suspicious of me. Now you are my real friend, aren't you?" She nodded emphatically and smiled.

If Del and Charlene keep searching, Our Jesus will keep nourishing that seed.

"Yes Coach, But"

Mabel had many financial, health, and family problems. Mabel knows the Lord, but it just doesn't seem to work for her. She had been in mental institutions several times. Jim, her husband, was also somewhat unstable. All this led to a messy home life. In spite of this, Mabel and Jim raised three excellent children who turned out well.

Mabel lived on pills and cigarettes. Jim wanted her to give up both, but she couldn't. Mabel constantly worried. She worried about everything all the time, and felt sorry for herself. She would call me or my wife frequently. She would also want to come over or have me come to her apartment to talk with her.

I encouraged her to consistently stay on God's program for her life which I had even outlined for her on paper. However, Mabel's conversation would be the same over and over.

"Coach, Jim is mistreating me, and he is going to beat me. I don't have any money to buy food or pills with next week. Do you think I should go to the mental hospital? What am I going to do if my car breaks down? Next month I will not have enough money to pay the rent. Where am I going when I get kicked out of here?"

I was concerned about Jim and Mabel. Both had suicidal tendencies. I kept encouraging them to go on a consistent spiritual program, insisting that if they did, our Lord would help them with all their problems.

"Mabel," I emphasized, "We must stay on God's spiritual program. We must read and hear about the Bible daily. We must communicate with Him many times a day. We must be with other Christians for strength, and we must serve Jesus. We must quit feeling sorry for ourselves. Mabel, self pity is the greatest destroyer of spirituality and our relationship with Jesus. We must think and be concerned about other people and other families who have the same problems we have."

"Yes, Coach, but I am running out of pills. I can't quit smoking. I won't have the rent money."

"Don't you trust Jesus, Mabel? Don't you know that if we turn our lives over to Jesus completely that He will take care of all our needs? He will open doors to make this possible!"

"Yes, Coach, but Jim is going to beat me, and how can I serve Jesus anyway?"

"Mabel, did you ever try going out to the nursing homes to read Bible stories and visit with people who need help much worse than you? If you do, when you come back you will praise God for how well off you really are. You won't feel the need to feel sorry for yourself."

"Yes, Coach, but how would I get out to the nursing home? I don't have any gas and my car is going to break down."

"Listen, Mabel," I exclaimed, "I don't want any more of your 'buts.' Just get on God's program, and stay there consistently. The 'buts' will take care of themselves. If you are not willing to help yourself do this, then I can't be of any help to you."

Mabel and Jim settled on a divorce. Praise God, Mabel obtained a job taking care of an elderly invalid. I believe this has really helped her stay closer to God as she has had to be concerned about someone else more than herself.

Jim and Mabel are now back together with their youngest daughter. God has given Mabel a new job she had wanted for years, and a new perspective. God has also eliminated the "buts" and most of her medicine from her life.

Jim and Mabel are just like other believers. If we stay consistently on God's spiritual program for our lives, God will give us a wonderful, fruitful, happy life. If we don't, God won't. I continue to pray for Jim and Mabel regularly, and remain available for further counseling.

Alcohol Quenches The Holy Spirit

"Take Pam home and bring her back when she is sober," I told Sally.

"Listen, mister," Pam interrupted, "I want you to know I am not drunk. I want to know now about this Jesus that you wrote about in your book."

"Take her home, Sally, and bring her back tomorrow afternoon if she is sobered up," I repeated. "I refuse to talk to her until she can understand what I am talking about."

"I can understand you now," Pam insisted. However, Sally agreed to take her home.

I had never met either Pam or Sally before. Both had read a book I wrote and decided that I could help Pam who was a chronic alcoholic. The next afternoon Sally brought Pam back, and she had not been drinking.

I told both Pam and Sally about Jesus, and they professed him. I emphatically told her that she would have to go on a definite, consistent spiritual program if she was going to get any help from God with her problem. I also invited her to Church and to weekly Bible studies.

Two weeks later Pam was in a sanitorium in a nearby city. She wrote to me, asking me to visit her. A week later I visited Pam, and I took her to Church services where I was speaking. When I left her that day, Pam seemed to be real close to God. She even asked me to tell one of her friends at the sanitorium about Jesus.

A short time later, Pam's ex-husband came to me with many problems. I had never met him before. Al professed Jesus, and started attending church and weekly Bible studies. Al also ended up in the sanitorium. I also talked to one of their daughters who accepted the Lord.

I am still concerned and I pray for each one regularly, but I have not contacted them. I believe before I can help them get closer to God, they need to willingly come back to God's program.

They know I am available if they make known their need. As believers, we must put God first in our lives, and follow His program if we are going to get help from God. Only then will Christianity work in our lives.

"There are three things that remain--
faith, hope, and love -- and the greatest
of these is love"
1 Corinthians 13:13

6

MINISTRY OF LOVE

I Need To Talk With You

"Dear Coach Eby: I am Theresa, a sixteen year old girl," the letter began. "I don't know you and you don't know me. I have read a copy of the book you wrote, 'Calling God's Tower.' Someone gave me a copy. I want you to know, Coach Eby, that I believe in God and I believe in Jesus. But after reading your book, I know that I have never had a personal encounter with Jesus. I have never joined the Family of God. I have never become a Christian. I need to talk with you!"
Sincerely, Theresa

"Dear Theresa: Thank you for your letter," I replied. "If it is OK with your parents, I will stop in to see you four weeks from this coming Sunday at 3:00 p.m. If your parents approve, tell me the directions to your home, and I will be there at the above appointed time."
Sincerely, Coach Eby

After receiving a letter of permission, I drove my car into Theresa's driveway right at 3:00 p.m. on the agreed day. As I got out of the car, a sixteen year old girl came out of the mobile home and said, "Hi, Coach Eby."

"Hi, Theresa," I answered.

It was the first time we had met, but already we were friends, because we had a common need of knowing Jesus.

However, Theresa was not there by herself. Coming out of the mobile home was Theresa's boy friend, her girl friend, her Mom and Dad, two brothers, and two cousins. After introductions, we all went back into the mobile home and sat on the living room floor and on different chairs. I told them

This 16 year old girl acted when God spoke and nine were saved including the above man, now her husband.

about the Bible and Jesus, and about God's Plan for each one of their lives. One hour later, all nine accepted Jesus and joined the family of God.

I wrote down all of the names and addresses, and gave each one of them two Bibles and a copy of my book. Just before leaving, we joined hands and had a circle prayer asking God's wonderful blessings upon my new friends and brothers and sisters in Christ.

Before I could leave three other teenagers came in who had

previously accepted Jesus, about a year before, in a crusade. They had heard that I was going to be at the mobile home and had dropped in to say hello.

After returning home, I called one of the teenagers: "Christy, this is Coach Eby. I am so happy you, Leo, and Sally dropped in. What about going down to that mobile home and ask if you, Leo, and Sally can start a weekly Bible Study? I am writing to tell them that I suggested you do this."

Christy promised that she would. I heard later that they were holding it each week on Thursday just as soon as the school bus got home.

Why did all of this happen? Not because of Coach Eby. I really didn't have anything to do with it. It happened because of the following three reasons: First, we have a wonderful, compassionate, loving God. Second, many people in that area had been praying for these people. Third, because a sixteen year old girl realized she wasn't right with God, and then had the courage to do something about it when God spoke to her.

Praise His Holy Name! I just happened to be present when God answered prayers and gave the increase as He sent the Holy Spirit into the hearts of nine people who chose the wonderful gift of God!

The last I knew, the nine were now attending church to be fed in the Word by Pastors, Sunday School teachers, and Christian friends.

Theresa and her boy friend, Larry, are now married. They have a beautiful baby who is being brought up in the nurture and admonition of the Lord in a Christian home.

Done Got Myself Pregnant

I was holding a crusade in a distant western state. I was doing door-to-door visitation with the local Pastor. At one house I was talking to a mother about Jesus when a 12th grade girl burst into the room from the outside.

I surmised that this was the mother's daughter, just coming home from school. I immediately went over to her and shook her hand. "I am Coach Eby from Coldwater, Michigan. What is your name?"

With a look of astonishment, she answered, "Katie."

"Are you any relation to this lady over here?" I asked.

"Yeh, that's my mother."

"I bet I can tell you your two hang-ups on Christianity, Katie."

"If you think you can, why don't you try?" she challenged me.

"Well, first of all, Katie, Christians have tried to cram it down your throat, isn't that right?"

"That's for sure, and I rebelled at that," she said.

"Katie, God doesn't do that. People do that. God gives everyone a free choice, so you can forget that hang-up," I explained.

"What is my other hang-up?" she countered.

"It is all the do's and don'ts people pushed at you along with Christianity," I volunteered. "Card playing, dancing, short skirts, smoking, etc. Am I right?"

"You sure are," she answered. "They want to tell me everything that I can do and can't do. This turns me off."

"Well, Katie, God doesn't do that either. People do. You don't have to please people. You and I have to please God."

With the hang-ups set aside, Katie was willing to listen to God's plan for her life. She accepted Jesus and joined the Family of God.

I was able to tell her how she and I needed to become a close friend of Jesus.

As we read and hear the Word, communicate with Him many times each day, be in fellowship with other children of God, and serve Jesus, Jesus through the Holy Spirit would come into our being in such strength, I told her, that it would change our lives and make it a blessing. If we just turn our lives over to Him and put God first in our lives, then God himself will take care of all the do's and don'ts.

A year later I received a telephone call from Katie, and she was crying.

"Coach, I done got myself pregnant."

I knew right then that Katie didn't need a scolding or chewing out. She needed the love of Jesus.

"Katie, I find no fault with you. I am concerned about you. I love you, and I want to be of help."

"I knew you would, Coach," she whimpered. "That's the reason I called you. What should I do, Coach?"

"Katie, it is just in a time like this that our Lord can and will help in a wonderful way.

"Katie, I want you to hang up on me, and sit down and write me a letter. I will sit down and write you a letter. Then let us both pray about this situation. As soon as you receive my letter you write me back and I will also answer your letter. Just remember, friend Katie, Our Lord wouldn't have you do anything foolish. After receiving your answer to my letter I will call you."

Three days later I received Katie's letter. "Dear Coach, please, please don't worry about me," she wrote. "I am going to be all right. I will not do anything foolish. I love the Lord Jesus, and I know I am in His Hands. I realize many women can't have children. I am going to keep my child as a gift from God. I thank you for your love and concern. Don't worry. I will be OK. Sincerely, Your sister in Christ, Katie."

Did God work it Out? Sure He did!

The Doctor was wrong. It was a false alarm.

A short time later a friend from Katie's church contacted me and told me how Katie had sung "The Holy City" in her church at Christmas time when she was home from college. He told me what a terrific job Katie did with that song.

Immediately I wrote to her and congratulated her on her singing and encouraged her to serve our Jesus in a like manner as often as possible.

Katie wrote back: "Coach, I really don't know if the people in the church enjoyed my singing or not, but I felt so filled with the Holy Spirit and felt so close to God while I was singing praises to Him."

Some time later I received another letter from Katie. She told me she had a new boy friend. He was really treating her like a lady and was so good to her.

"Coach, there is no more of that other going on. God is in control." Six months later I received an invitation to Katie's wedding.

God's ministry is a ministry of love, not criticism and judgment. People can fight criticism but they can't fight the love of Jesus!

I Have My Own Religion

I was conducting a week of meetings in Columbus, Ohio. One morning as I was eating breakfast in the hotel dining room, I was asked a question by a young man at an adjacent table.

He asked me the time, and we chatted back and forth a few minutes. I picked up my coffee and went over to his table and, with his permission, I sat down. We introduced ourselves.

Dave was twenty years old, and had left college to go world traveling. He had just returned to the states from Africa. He had spent all his money, and now was in need of a job. His Dad was a scientist at the University of Cincinnati. Dave's Dad had come from a poverty stricken home life, and had worked himself up to an important position as a scientist. Dave's father was really disgusted with his son for not bearing down and making something of himself. He thought Dave was crazy to spend his money and time traveling all over the world.

Dave and I soon became friends as we chatted back and forth. I gave him a copy of the Bible and a copy of my book.

"Now listen Coach, I like you and you are my friend, but don't try handing me any of this stuff. I have my own religion."

"Yes, Dave what is it?"

"I believe in reincarnation," Dave emphatically stated.

I said much louder this time, "What did you say, Dave?"

Dave almost shouted back, "I said I believe in reincarnation!"

Many people in the dining room were now looking at our table.

I doubled my fists and threw both of my arms in the air and shouted back, "That is great. That is marvelous. That is tremendous. That is terrific, Dave!"

"It is?" Dave asked, with an incredible look on his face.

"Yes, Dave, it is great that you believe in something. But wouldn't you like to know what happened to me and my wife?"

I presumed this sounded interesting to Dave, and he answered, "Yeh."

I then proceeded to tell him how my wife and I came to know the Lord. In about forty minutes Dave had professed Jesus and joined the Family of God.

I told Dave that he could stay in my hotel room with me that night, and it wouldn't cost him a cent. I called the desk to let them know to charge me for an extra person.

However, Dave decided to take a bus to Akron, Ohio. His Dad and Mom were split, but when he called his mother, she told him that Dave's father was spending the weekend at her home in Akron. Dave boarded the bus. I said goodbye to him, and I told him I would write to him if he would let me know his address.

Later in the afternoon, as I was making final preparations for that night's meeting, there was a knock on my hotel room door. I opened it, and there stood Dave. He was about to cry.

"Come on in Dave, and sit down. It's good to see you again."

Dave related that as his Dad and Mom met him at the bus station, they notified him that they never wanted to see him again. Not knowing what to do, he brought the bus back to

Columbus and to the hotel. I invited him to stay with me for the weekend, and I told him I would take care of his expenses.

Dave went with me to the meeting that evening in Columbus. It was a large meeting of Christian men. I was the speaker. I introduced Dave to everyone who came in as my new brother in Christ. I didn't know most of the men myself, but we were soon acquainted.

Dave was a chain smoker and this was the type of a meeting where people did not smoke. I told Dave that during the meal and program to leave at any time to go out into the hall and have a smoke. No one would care.

God further touched Dave's heart during the fellowship and the message. Back in our hotel room, Dave confessed to me.

"Coach, I had more love shown to me tonight by all strangers than I had shown to me by my parents all the time I lived at home. It is just incredible. I just can't believe it. They all treated me like they had loved me all my life. I am gratified, and I am astonished."

"Dave, these men are not strangers. Every one of them is your brother in Christ, and they do love you. That is what this new way of life is all about."

Dave and I laid in our respective beds and talked about this new way of life until 2:00 in the morning.

"I have to get some sleep, Dave," I finally told him. "I have to get up at 5:00 to go to a prayer breakfast. You will be sleeping in."

"No, I won't," he answered. "I will be going with you."

At the prayer breakfast, Dave took his turn at reading the scripture. His portion was the scripture about becoming a new creature in Christ. Praise God. It was thrilling to have Dave next to me on his knees praying to our Father in Heaven.

I don't believe in arguing about Jesus. I think it is absurd and silly to think that I have to defend the Bible and Jesus. I believe arguing with people turns them off and doesn't accomplish a thing.

I could have argued with Dave about reincarnation, and I could have shown him scriptures about it. But I believe that we could still have been arguing about it. I didn't say that I believed in reincarnation, I just said it was marvelous that he believed in something.

I then immediately told him how my wife and I had our lives changed completely by Jesus, and I explained to him what an exciting life we are now living.

Don't argue about Jesus. Just tell people and let them see what Jesus has done for you!

I Have Something To Tell You Coach

A twenty year old local girl called me and wanted to rent a mobile home. I met Pam at the mobile home, took her deposit, and gave her a receipt. Just as we were leaving the mobile home, Pam shuffled up close to me and sort of whispered, "I have something to tell you Coach. My boy friend is going to live with me part of the time."

Six months before I would have told Pam, "Take your junk and move. I don't rent to scum."

Praise God, He has changed me and I said to Pam, "That is between you and God and it is none of my business."

Phil moved in completely and permanently with Pam.

For a year and a half, Pam and Phil were good tenants. Every time I met them, I treated them with the love of Jesus, just as nice as I possibly could.

After eighteen months they moved out and purchased a mobile home of their own. Six months later Pam called me. "Coach, would you marry Phil and me?"

"I don't know, Pam Why don't you and Phil come over and rap with me first. Perhaps after talking to me, you won't want me to marry you. Perhaps I won't want to marry you. Just come over and let us find out."

Phil and Pam came over and I told them about God's plan for their lives. Both of them accepted Jesus and joined the

Received Jesus while in a motel room, from crime to serving Jesus.

Family of God. I married them as one in Christ.

I could have turned them out of the mobile home for living together, and I would have turned them off on Jesus. Whether we like it or not, we, as believers, represent Jesus. We need to continually radiate the love of Jesus and let God do the judging.

Some people might say that I condone this way of living by allowing it to go on. Nonsense. Pam and Phil knew how I felt about it. Only God changes people. I praise God that because of His Love, I was able to see Pam and Phil come to the Lord.

You Can Just Keep Your Church

As I was having meetings in Florida, I met a young lady who was the receptionist at the motel I was staying in. I started talking to Rena in the motel office about the Bible and Jesus. Several others came in and joined the group.

Rena interrupted my remarks.

"Coach, I was raised in a family of atheists. About two years ago, a minister told me about Jesus and I professed

Him. I went to Sunday School for the first time. The lady teaching the class asked me my name and introduced me to the class asking me to stand up. 'We are really happy to have you with us, Rena,' the teacher said. 'We would like to have you come back each week. However, young lady, before you come back next week, we want you to remove those earrings, and the rouge and lipstick'."

"You know what I told her, Coach?" Rena asked.

"I can guess," I answered.

Rena said, "I told her that she could keep her blank church, and I walked out and never went back. Some time later one of my relatives died, and I took my Bible with me to the funeral. I was really scorned and ridiculed by all my atheist relatives. I just wonder if it isn't easier just to remain being an atheist."

Oh, if we could only remember to never judge or ridicule people. Just show them the love of Jesus, and let Him change their lives as we encourage them to get close to God.

A Tip For The Waitress

"Dear Coach Eby, I am writing you this letter to let you know that about a year ago you were eating in the restaurant where I was working as a waitress. I am sure you don't remember me, but as a tip you gave me a copy of a book you wrote, 'Calling God's Tower'. I took it home and started reading it, but decided that I didn't want any of that stuff. I put it away on a shelf. About two months ago I picked it up and started reading it again. I found it fascinating, and I really feel the presence of God. I know I need to know Him personally. Can you help me? Sincerely, Mary Beth."

Some time later I was flying my plane late at night from Toledo, Ohio, toward Kentucky. I was having trouble with some thunderstorms, and decided to stay overnight in a southern Indiana city where I had some special friends. As I landed at 2:00 in the morning, they picked me up at the airport and took me to a motel.

A tip to a waitress - God brought the increase.

The next morning Bill and Debbie picked me up at the motel and took me to a prayer breakfast. After the breakfast, God reminded me that Mary Beth lived in this same town. I asked Bill and Debbie if they knew where Mary Beth lived. They drove me out to Mary Beth's house.

I knocked on the door and a sixteen year old girl opened it. "I bet you are Mary Beth."

"I am sure you are Coach Eby," she answered.

Mary Beth invited me in and said that her folks were in Florida. We sat down at a kitchen table, and I presented her with a couple of Bibles. As we started talking about Jesus, a tall young man walked into the kitchen. Mary Beth introduced me to her brother, Mike, who was attending a nearby University. Before I left, both of them accepted Jesus and joined the Family of God.

Praise God for a Saviour who opens doors in such marvelous ways and allows us to be around sometimes when He gives the increase.

No Prejudice In The Family of God

After giving a message in a college, several young men and ladies came to see me about getting right with God. Larinda was a small black girl who was now excited about being right with God. Later I received the following letter from her.

"Dear Coach Eby, Hello in the name of Jesus. I pray that this letter finds you and your family in good health and truly praising the Lord and Saviour, our Jesus Christ. I just want to thank you for the letter that you sent. It meant a lot to me. The Bible studies are just wonderful. I need to look up these scriptures as much as possible. I am glad you are a child of God and myself too. I am glad that we are in one family, *the Family of God!*

"Please don't forget me. God Bless you, Love in Christ, Larinda."

Under God, how could I ever possibly be prejudiced against a wonderful sister in Christ like Larinda just because of the color of her skin. I love her and we are one in Christ!

My Daughter Is Driving Me Crazy

On the final night of the crusade, a couple came to me. "Coach, would you talk to our sixteen year old daughter. She is a mess."

"I would be happy to on one condition - that she wants to talk with me. Where is she?"

"Cathy was at the meeting and she heard your message," the father volunteered. "She is now across the street in the car. I will go over and tell her that you are going to talk to her."

"No," I interrupted, "I will go over to the car."

When I reached the middle of the street, Cathy came to me and threw her arm around me and started whimpering. I didn't know Cathy but I knew the family slightly, and I knew the parents were Christians.

"Cathy, what about you and me going to my house and

getting right with God. Is that all right?"

She answered yes.

Cathy and I went back into the church and approached her parents. "Don, with your permission, Cathy and I are going to my house and get right with God. Why don't both of you come with my wife and wait in our living room. We will be down in our recreation room."

After Cathy accepted Jesus, we went upstairs to the living room where Cathy's parents and my wife were visiting. I went over and sat down on the davenport and Cathy followed me and sat next to me.

Cathy's mother started telling me, "Coach Eby, this daughter of mine is driving me crazy. I can't take any more of it. She is driving me up the wall. You know what happened to my oldest daughter, and the same thing will happen to Cathy if she keeps on running around with that long haired bum. If this keeps on, I will end up in a mental institution."

"Mrs. Jones, perhaps I should talk to you about Jesus, and show you how you can turn these problems over to Him," I said. "Cathy is now right with God, aren't you, Cathy?"

She nodded.

"God is going to change Cathy as only God can. You or your husband cannot change Cathy."

"I would like to talk to Sam, Cathy's boyfriend."

The mother interrupted, "We forbid her to go with him."

"That is your privilege," I continued. "I will not argue, but I do not know Sam. The chances of Sam coming to see me without Cathy is nil. Perhaps Cathy can convince Sam to come with her."

The parents conceded to allow this.

The next evening Cathy brought Sam to my office in my home. He was very suspicious and much on guard. I soon made friends with him and told him about Jesus. He professed Jesus, and all three of us ended up with a circle prayer. I gave him a Bible and followed up with both Sam and Cathy.

God is good. I married this family's oldest daughter to a fine Christian and together they are a fine Christian couple much used of God. This family's oldest boy came back home and got right with God. Sam and Cathy seemed to get along well with each other.

Truly, these parents were good Christian parents. The rules in their home for their children were probably about the same as in our household. We Christian parents need to know that our rules and restrictions must be administered in the love of Jesus at all times.

Bride is used of God to bring her husband to Jesus before the wedding.

Children recognize when we don't use the love of Jesus in enforcing His guidelines even if we don't realize it ourselves at the time. We parents also must realize that our job is completed, whether we like it or not, when our children become teenagers. Only God will change them after that. It is so important that we bring our children up in the nurture and admonition of the Lord when they are young. If we do, they are more apt to survive when the crises come.

My Girl Friend Says I Am Not Religious Enough

Rob called me and set up an appointment. We didn't know each other but he had a problem.

"Coach Eby, I am in love with Jan, and I want to marry her. Jan tells me that I am not religious enough for her. What does she mean, Coach?"

Rob and I went to the Bible. Rob accepted Jesus and joined the Family of God. Now Rob and Jan have really come alive in Jesus.

They attend church and a weekly Bible study regularly. Both are being used of God as a witness for Him in their everyday life. They hand out Christian literature and talk to people and encourage them to walk with Jesus.

In a few short weeks, I am going to have the privilege of marrying Rob and Jan as one in Christ. I just know their marriage will be happy and that it will have a real influence for other couples.

I praise God for girls like Jan who refuse to be unequally yoked, but who are willing to be used of God to be a witness to their boy friend to the saving knowledge of our Lord Jesus.

I Don't Have A Bible

Martha wrote me a letter stating that she had read a copy of my book, "Calling God's Tower." Although we didn't know each other, she felt that I could help her.

Martha and her husband had five children. According to Martha she had gone through several years of hell on earth. Her husband was a heavy drinker, and had beaten her up many times. Even her older boys were now beating her up when she tried to discipline them. I wrote back and made some spiritual suggestions.

A few weeks later, on a Monday morning, I was leaving the house for a six hour drive for meetings in Martha's area. Before I left the house, Martha called me on the phone. She had heard that I was having meetings for a week in her area, and she wanted to see me. I told Martha that I would be in a certain motel in a certain town at 7:00 p.m. that night.

Martha had indicated in her letter that she was a Christian but her husband wasn't. At 7:00 p.m., Martha and her 5th grade daughter, Sharon, knocked on my motel room door.

I let them in and introduced myself and asked them to sit down. Martha started telling me about her problems. Because of the beatings, and strain of an uptight environment, she had spent several terms in a mental institution.

I interrupted her. "You sure you are a Christian."

"Oh yes," she answered. "I made a decision for Jesus when I was young."

"You are really sure then, Martha, that you have had a personal encounter with Jesus, and have no doubts about belonging to the Family of God?"

She said she was sure.

I started discussing her problems like she was a Christian, but something just didn't seem to ring true.

"Martha, how much do you read the Bible?"

She looked at me, astonished, and remarked, "I don't have a Bible."

"Oh, come on, Martha, let us get down to the 'nitty gritty'. You really don't know Jesus, do you?"

She then confirmed my suspicion.

"Let us open up the Bible and make sure that Coach, Martha, and Sharon are right with God," I suggested.

I gave both of them Bibles. We read and discussed the salvation verses, and took the three necessary steps to accept Jesus and joined the Family of God. Now Martha and Sharon can receive help from our Lord.

We discussed how Jesus could help us with our problems. At 8:00 p.m. six men came to my motel room to pray for the next day's meetings. I introduced all of them to my two new sisters in Christ, Martha and Sharon. All nine of us joined hands and had a circle prayer asking God's blessing upon our two new sisters.

I followed up with personal letters and Bible courses. The other men and wives followed up for fellowship in Christian groups for Martha and Sharon. Martha and Sharon drove 150 miles each night for two nights to attend the meetings I was speaking at. We had a grand fellowship. I pray that I will get to see them again personally soon.

We must remember that before we can receive help from God, we first must know Him personally!

An airplane ride and then through Jesus became my sister in Christ.

"Pray ye therefore the Lord of the harvest, that He will send forth labourers into His harvest."
Matthew 9:38

7

SPREADING THE GOOD NEWS

Just One Ninth Grade Girl

"Coach Eby, I want to talk with you; I want to get right with God." Dawn was a ninth grade girl who came to me after the morning worship service in a church in northern Indiana.

"That's just great, Dawn. You have made my day, coming to me! Come on in this room and you and I will 'rap' and get right with God."

I gave Dawn two Bibles and a copy of my book. I opened up the Bible and we went through the salvation verses. Dawn accepted the three necessary steps to join the Family of God, and she became my sister in Christ.

Just one ninth grade girl, you might say. This one ninth grade girl went home and had her entire family of Dad and Mom and six brothers and sisters come back to the noon church potluck. Dawn introduced me to every member of her family, and I made friends with them.

After the potluck, the entire family stayed for the mid-afternoon service. As they left the church, I asked Dad if I could come out to their mobile home and visit with them. He agreed. As I visited them that afternoon, Dad and Mom, and five brothers and sisters came to know Jesus and joined the Family of God. The baby was too young.

One year later I was in the same church for a one-day crusade. Dawn's entire family was in church and had been attending faithfully all year. Dad and Mom were singing in the choir, and Dawn was helping with a Sunday School class. Dawn also brought her boy friend to me who accepted Jesus.

Since then, the entire family has visited meetings where I was speaking in order to fellowship together. This entire family has been precious to me as we have corresponded and visited each other.

Yes, just one ninth grade girl. But, oh, how God has and is using her! Because of an all-compassionate God, prayers by other Christians, and one girl who did something about it when God spoke to her, a family became united in Jesus Christ!

Jesus On The Phone

A couple whom I didn't know came to me in my office. "Coach Eby, would you please read this letter?"

"Dear Mom and Dad," the letter went. "I have had a terrible auto accident, and I am in a hospital here in Tennessee. I really am in bad shape and I am afraid I am not going to make it. I am scared and don't know what to do. I am afraid to die. I heard of a man called Coach Eby. I don't know him but you must know him as he is from Coldwater. Would you please contact him and have him get in touch with me? Sincerely, Your son, Dale."

"Coach," the parents pleaded, "Will you at least call him on the phone?"

"That would not do any good," I answered. "There is

nothing Coach Eby can do for Dale with or without the phone. We three are going to have a prayer session right now. We are going to pray that God will send the Holy Spirit right now ahead of the phone call, and will prepare Dale's heart for what he needs."

After a session of prayer, I picked up the phone and called the hospital who connected me with Dale in his room. Fifteen minutes later Dale gave his heart to Jesus as I talked to him on the phone.

I received several letters from Dale telling how our Lord was helping him in so many ways. Dale has passed from death unto life. He also recovered physically. Praise the Holy Name of Jesus!

Finding Life Worth Living

"Coach Eby, you don't know me. I am Jane and I decided to call you. My cousin Brenda is pregnant and she is threatening to commit suicide. Would you please come over and talk with her?"

I jumped into my car and followed her directions to her home.

I introduced myself to the two twenty year old girls. I gave them both Bibles, and through the scriptures I showed them how God could make life worth living. Both Jane and Brenda accepted Jesus, and became my sisters in Christ.

Jane's mother was having problems in her second marriage. Jane directed both of them, Rose and Jim, to me. They also became children of God. In the factory in which Rose worked was a twenty year old girl, Christi. Christi came into work one morning looking so depressed that Rose gave her my telephone number, and suggested she call me. Christi called and also came over and became my sister in Christ.

Christi started attending my weekly Bible Study. Her life started changing rapidly. Her mother called me and said she couldn't understand what was changing her daughter since

Problems brought her to the foot of the cross.

she started attending my meetings.

As she thanked me, I interrupted, "Don't thank me. I had nothing to do with it. God did all the changing."

Each Wednesday night at Bible Study, Christi would "bug" me about going up to Detroit and see her Aunt who was ill and needed Jesus.

"Christi, I will see if your Aunt wishes to see me as soon as God opens the door by placing me in that area." Every time I saw Christi, she would remind me to see Aunt Bertha. This kept it fresh on my mind and I prayed about it.

I flew to Appleton, Wisconsin, to speak on Thursday night. On Friday, I flew back to Battle Creek, picked up my car and drove to Flint for two days of meetings. On Sunday morning I drove to Detroit, and after the service the Pastor invited me to dinner.

"Coach, you have time to come eat and have fellowship with our family before you start for Adrian and tonight's speaking commitment."

"Just let me make one call first, Pastor. I will soon know God's schedule for me this afternoon." God had brought to mind Christi's Aunt Bertha.

Aunt Bertha answered the phone. "Bertha, this is Coach Eby, and you don't know me."

She answered, "Christi has told me about you."

"Bertha, I have just enough time to drive over to your house and visit you before I start for Adrian for a Sunday evening service. However, I will not come unless you ask me to. I will not talk to anyone about this new way of life unless they want me to. You just say the word, Bertha, come or don't."

"I wish you would come," she answered. "I want to see you."

I knew right then that Bertha was going to accept Jesus. She indicated with her invitation that God through the Holy Spirit had already been there and prepared her heart.

I then turned down the Pastor's invitation for dinner and fellowship. After I spent an hour with Bertha, we were both in the same Family of God. Praise God the way He can use a chain of contacts starting with my friend, Jane. Just recently Jane's boyfriend has also accepted Jesus.

Hey You, Those Are Mine

As I was having a series of meetings in Tulsa, Oklahoma, I found time to spend a couple of hours witnessing in a Tulsa recreational park. I took some Bibles and books with me and placed some of them on a low brick wall where people were walking past.

I then asked the Lord to lead me to someone that He had already prepared. As I walked around the park, I noticed a middle aged lady talking to a teenage boy. They were really having problems and I felt led to contact them.

"Friends, I am Coach Eby from Coldwater, Michigan. Are you from Tulsa?"

"No, we are from Kansas," the lady answered.

"Well," I replied, "I have just been visiting here in this park. I have found a new way of life that is just tremendous. It doesn't cost a cent, and it will take care of all of our problems. Would you want to hear about it?"

They were willing. The lady and her sixteen year old son listened to God's plan for their lives and professed Jesus. I took their names and addresses so I could write to them.

I walked back to where I had left my Bibles and books, and two teenage girls were picking them up and looking at them. I shouted at them, "Hey you, those are mine!"

They immediately put them down, and one of them said, "We weren't going to take them. We were just looking at them."

"Oh that is all right," I cheerfully answered. "I am going to give them to you free."

I wrote their names in Bibles and books which I presented to them. We sat down at a picnic table and I told them about Jesus. Both of them professed Christ.

In two hours I talked to 25 people in the park, and gave out Bibles and books. People were always available to be approached because someone would be curiously looking at my stack of Bibles and books.

I only had time to make complete presentations to six, all of whom professed Jesus. However, none of the other nineteen objected to me talking to them about this new way of life. This is a great time to be a Christian. People are really searching for something good, and only God is good.

A Flight To Jesus

Two of my friends, man and wife, were telling me about their oldest son.

"Coach, Chip is married and he and his wife have three beautiful children. He is going to school at a southern university. He and his family are here at home for the summer. We asked him the other day if he had ever accepted Jesus as his personal Saviour. He said no. We feel bad because we tried to bring him up in the nurture and admonition of the Lord. We wonder if you could talk with him?"

"What is Chip's main interest?" I asked. "Is he interested in flying at all?"

The parents informed me that he was taking up aeronautics at the University.

"Well, friends, you tell Chip that in four weeks I am flying to a Christian fly-in where I am to speak. Be sure to inform him that this is a Christian oriented trip including some church services. If he wants to go with me, he is welcome, and it won't cost him a cent."

I guess Chip's thrill of flying and his interest in aviation overbalanced the fact that he would have to spend three days with a Jesus fanatic. He had never met me but of course he had heard about me. He decided to go with me anyway.

Four weeks later we flew to the fly-in at an airport in southern Indiana. After a Friday night of Christian fellowship, on Saturday Chip met many Christian pilots and also sat through the messages I was giving.

On Saturday night we flew to Bloomington, Indiana, and stayed in a motel together. We spent at least four hours talking about Jesus, but I did not ask him to make a decision. I kept everything on a friendly basis. I made sure that I didn't push him.

The next day I had three messages in a Bloomington church. I knew that God was speaking to Chip. At the Sunday evening service, three of my close friends drove to Bloomington to worship with us. They came early and Chip and I were visiting with them.

"Hey friends, what about all five of us going downstairs, and having a circle prayer for the services tonight?"

The four followed me downstairs where we joined hands and prayed for God's blessings on the evening service. Chip was the only one who didn't pray, but he was really squeezing my hand tight as we others prayed. During the service I could tell that Chip was a new creature in Christ. He was praising God inside and out!

Chip and his wife, Irma, and children, are real precious to me. Later on when I was having a special crusade in their area, they came nightly to the meetings, praising God.

He Doesn't Like You

A friend of mine asked me to look up his brother-in-law and wife who lived in a nearby city.

"Coach, they both need to get right with God. I believe you might be the man to talk to them. I can't. I need to warn you that Art knows about you and doesn't like you. Somebody told him that you were involved in a shady business deal where you took advantage of a person. He is looking for some reason to dislike you even though he doesn't know you."

I told my friend, "Terry, I wish I knew about that deal; I don't remember any such deal."

Certain people are always trying to tear down a Christian's testimony. I personally do not worry about it. My God is a great God and is not limited. If my motives are Christlike, then no way can people hurt me. If I say they can then I am admitting that my God is limited.

I told Terry I would make contact with the family and see if God would open the door.

I stopped twice at their house, and I met Art's wife and a couple of children. Art was not at home either time. I did nothing more about it. I thought it wasn't God's accepted time or I wasn't the right person.

Some time later, I was speaking at a prayer breakfast meeting in a nearby city. After the message several people came up to speak to me. The last one was Art.

He introduced himself. "Coach Eby, I am Art and my wife and I have read your book. We decided to come hear you speak this morning. My wife was here for the message but she had to leave early to go to work. God touched our hearts this morning and sometime we would like to talk to you.

I believe that word "sometime" is of the devil. When I arrived home I immediately looked up my calendar of commitments, and called Art. I suggested a certain date, and Art vowed that he and his wife would be there. At this meeting, Art and his wife got right with God.

What a tremendous Christian couple they are now. I have been in Bible Studies where God is using Art's leadership ability. Both of them have really enriched my life with their Christian fellowship and friendship. Praise God who can bring any or all people together!

From a commune to Jesus.

Language Barrier

As I was having a week of meetings in Eagle Pass, Texas, right on the Mexican border, my service was at an American Mexican Baptist Church. Upon arrival at the church I was introduced to the Pastor who couldn't speak English, and I couldn't speak Spanish. I located the associate pastor and found out that he could speak both. He told me that they planned to use a lady as my interpreter.

I asked him how many people in the church could understand English.

He answered, "All of our young people can understand

both English and Spanish. Some of our older folks can understand Spanish only."

"Could I speak to the entire group in English, then give another short message that the lady can interpret into Spanish?" I asked. "I believe the communication to the young people directly will be so much more effective." They agreed.

As I gave the first message, God really had the attention of the young people. Some of the older people were somewhat restless not being able to understand a word I was saying.

The lady did a good job of interpreting my second message which everybody could understand. Some of my terminology about flying sometimes gave her trouble.

Nevertheless, God touched the hearts of nineteen teenagers who came to me after the meeting and got right with Jesus. What a blessing it was to write and send Bible Courses to these wonderful young people who were excited about having a personal relationship with Jesus!

From Prison To A Child Of The King

I received a phone call from Mary and Joe. I didn't know them, but they were living together in a hotel room. They asked me if I would come to the hotel room and talk with them.

After Mary and Joe answered my knock on the door, I went in and sat down. I gave them Bibles and told them about God's Wonderful Plan for their lives. Mary and Joe both professed Jesus. A few days later the hotel burned, killing a man. But Mary's and Joe's room was the only room that did not burn inside. They had been protected from both smoke and flames.

Joe and Mary were inconsistent about following God's spiritual program. They soon split, and their problems continued. Mary had to spend several months in a prison for a crime she had committed before she was saved.

Sometime after Mary's release, she started being serious about following God's program. I am happy to report that she is now real close to her Saviour. She attends weekly Bible Study and church. She reads the Bible regularly, and is bringing her three beautiful children up in the nurture and admonition of the Lord. Mary just looks great as Jesus shines through her life. Mary will continue to have this wonderful life if she continues to put God first in her life as much as she possibly can. Mary has learned the truth of *Galatians 6:9 "And let us not get tired of doing what is right for after a while we will reap a harvest of blessing if we don't get discouraged and give up."*

Joe, as many of us, needs to discipline himself to follow the program.

I Hate People

The phone rang. "Coach Eby, this is Michele. You don't know me, but I need to talk with you. Would you please come to my house?"

After introductions Michele told me her problem. Michele was married to Roger and together they had four children. When Brett was nine months old and creeping, the family was vacationing at the lake. Brett was crawling around on the yard, and Michele and Roger had agreed that both of them would keep an eye on him.

Unfortunately little Brett drowned in the lake. Michele blamed herself and her husband. She was angry at her husband, and carried a guilt complex around with her at all times. This resulted in hate for people, suicide attempts, and mental illness followed by treatment at mental institutions. Michele was unhappy, unstable, and hateful. She was continually having trouble with neighbors and all other people with whom she came in contact. Michele felt everyone was picking on her and treating her unjustly.

The day I first met Michele I opened the Bible and told her about the love of Jesus. Michele accepted Jesus, and joined the Family of God. She started reading the Bible and attending weekly Bible Studies. Michele's life started changing slowly but gradually. She couldn't understand why things didn't get better quicker. I kept trying to encourage her through all her ups and downs.

Recently, Michele called me with great excitement. "Praise the Lord, Coach Eby. Isn't He just wonderful? God has finally come alive in my life. I just feel wonderful. I don't hate anyone any more. I love everybody. I feel so close to Jesus. I am not depressed any more. Jesus just feels so close at all times, and I can call on Him any time. Thank you, Jesus!"

My friend Michele found out what it is all about. She now knows for sure that when we completely surrender our lives to Jesus and put Him first in our life, He will give us a wonderful, exciting life.

The Important Business First

I was renting a house I owned in a nearby city to one of my former students. Mabel called me and told me she was moving. However, she had another lady that wanted to rent the home. I agreed to meet Mabel at the airport.

She picked me up and drove me over to the house. Mabel introduced me to the lady, Katie, and her teenage daughter, Carrie. Katie immediately told me she had the deposit, and wanted to rent the house.

I interrupted. "Let us take up some important business first! If you and Carrie are willing, I would like to tell you about a wonderful new way of life that is exciting and helpful." They agreed to listen. There was no furniture in the house at the time.

"Why don't we sit down on this carpet in the living room and relax?"

Mabel, who was already a Christian also sat down on the living room floor with us. I gave them Bibles, and went through God's Plan of Salvation. Both Katie and Carrie professed Jesus, and of course Mabel helped lead the way by agreeing to the necessary steps.

Right after I prayed for them and said Amen, Carrie, the teenager, ran out of the house and jumped into the car, and took off. As I was closing the rental deal, Carrie came back in with her boyfriend.

She simply stated, "Please tell Jack about Jesus."

Be Not Unequally Yoked

During one of my crusades, the organist was an eighteen year old senior named Doris. After the morning worship service, we had a potluck dinner at the church. At the dinner I sat across the table from Doris' parents. Doris had introduced me to her boy friend, Ted.

Doris' parents were concerned, because she planned to marry Ted in the fall. Ted came from a non-Christian home, with no Christian training. The church and Jesus had never been part of their lives. Naturally, Doris' parents were somewhat uptight about her marrying an unbeliever. Doris had coaxed Ted into coming to church that morning to hear the special speaker.

"Coach Eby," Doris' father spoke, "We wish you would talk to Ted."

I agreed to be alert to see if God would open the door. As I was driving around town that Sunday afternoon making calls, I spotted Ted and Doris passing me with Ted's car. I honked and waved them over to the side of the road. I jumped out of my car and hurried over to Ted's side of the car.

"Hey friends, I have just heard some great news. I heard you two are getting married this fall. Isn't that just great?"

Both of them beamed with joy.

"You know," I continued, "We three should sit down together and have a rap session. I have some great things to tell you that can assure you of a happy marriage. What about it, Ted, would you be willing?"

From a church crusade to one in Christ in marriage.

He said yes, and naturally Doris also agreed.

"You pick the time, Ted and Doris, while I am here these three days."

That night, after the service, Ted and Doris came to me and asked to talk with me. We spent a wonderful hour together, as we made sure that we were all right with God according to the scriptures. We all ended up brothers and sister in Christ.

Ted came to every service and sat by himself until Doris was through playing the organ. At the commitment service on the last night, Ted was one of the first to stand up and publicly commit his life to a life of service to Jesus.

Recently, Ted and Doris drove over to my house to have fellowship with me. We went flying together, but more important we worshiped together. We three have found a real personal relationship with each other through Jesus Christ. I just love Ted and Doris, and my Jesus who gave them to me as a brother and sister in Christ!

Ted and Doris are now married, one in Christ.

> *"And he said, The things which are*
> *impossible with men are possible*
> *with God."*
> *Luke 18:27*

MIRACLES FROM GOD

It Won't Work

As I was having meetings in Columbus, Ohio, a friend of mine, the father of one of my former students, came to me. "Coach, my daughter, Sue, whom you had in school is now living in Columbus. She has been divorced and has a daughter, Norma. She is living a messy life, and has many problems. Would you visit her while you are in Columbus?" He gave me her address and I decided to make contact.

I rang the doorbell, and Sue opened her apartment door. She recognized me. "Hi, Coach, won't you come in?"

I stepped in and sat down. "Sue, I understand you are having some problems. I would like to tell you about Jesus who can help you with those problems."

"Listen, Coach, you were my former teacher, and I like you. But I have my own religious belief, and it is not based on the Bible."

"I won't argue with you, Sue, and I will leave. Could I say just one more thing before I leave?"

"Certainly, Coach, go ahead."

"It won't work," I said, and left!

Eight months later I received a phone call from a jail in the Columbus Ohio, area. It was Sue and she was crying. "Coach Eby, this is Sue. I have been in this jail for two weeks, and it is driving me buggy. I am ready to climb the walls. I just can't stand it another day in this jail. I have to get out today, and go home and see my daughter, Norma. Would you please come down here and get me out of this jail?"

It is necessary to relate why my friend, Sue, was in jail. She had enticed an elderly gentleman to put her in his will for one-half of his total estate upon his death. Then she decided that she didn't want to wait until his natural death. She hired a "hit man" for ten thousand dollars to "bump" the man off. She borrowed five hundred dollars from the elderly gentleman to give to the hit man as a down payment for the job. The hit man was going to have to perform the job, and then wait until the will was probated before he received the balance.

With five hundred dollars in one pocket and a gun in the other, the hit man went off to perform the job. When he came to the elderly gentleman, fortunately, the hit man lost his courage, and broke down and confessed to the man. Both of them went to the police, and broke the story.

A plain clothes policeman went back to Sue with the original hit man. The hit man said to Sue, "I lost my courage and I can't do it. Here is your five hundred dollars. My friend here will do it for ten thousand dollars. Give him the five hundred down payment."

Sue handed the five hundred over to the plain clothesman. Naturally, they had her nailed, and threw her in jail.

"No way, Sue, am I interested in getting you out of jail. I wouldn't get you out of jail even if I could. No way!"

"I thought you would want to help me," Sue whimpered.

"No way, Sue, but if you invite me to, I will be happy to drive down and tell you about Jesus who can help you!"

"Would you do that, Coach?" Sue asked.

"I sure will," I agreed.

That night as I was having Bible Studies in Coldwater, I told my Christian friends about the problems my friend Sue was having.

In each one of my studies, someone would speak up. "Coach, we don't know Sue, but we love her. We want to pray that God will turn her life around like He is doing for us." So we prayed for Sue in each Bible Study.

Totally blind but God brought 20-20 spiritual vision.

The next day I made the long trip to the jail. With the permission of the sheriff, I was able to take Sue into a private room where there was just Sue, the Holy Spirit, and me. I gave her a Bible, and we went through God's plan for our lives. You know what brought Sue to the foot of the cross and gave her the real desire to accept Jesus? It was when I told her that people in my home town who didn't even know her, loved her and were praying for her. This brought her face to face with Jesus.

After praying with Sue, I explained to her. "Sue, if you are sincere about your profession, and I believe you are, you are no longer under the control of the courts, judges, lawyers, and jailer. You are now under the control of Jesus Christ. You don't need to be concerned about bail, trials, evidence, or lawyers. Sue, I must tell you that you will not get out of this jail or any other jail until God wants you out. I don't know when. And it may be a long time before He sees fit to release you. But I can tell you this, Sue, when God wants you out, there is nothing that can keep you in!

"If you don't believe this, Sue, you go to Acts Chapter 12 of the Bible and read about Peter. Peter was thrown into jail. Soldiers were placed on each side of him. He was in a locked cell with chains on his wrists. Believers were praying for Peter's release just like believers are praying for your release, Sue. The soldiers fell asleep and an angel told Peter to stand up. As he did, the chains fell off his wrist. As he walked up to the iron gate, it opened of its own accord. Peter walked out a free man.

"Sue, if you really mean business with the Lord, He can and will do the same thing for you at the accepted time."

"I really mean it, Coach," Sue answered. "I am turning my life over to Jesus."

The next week, Sue's lawyer, a public defender, came to her. "Sue, you must give me permission to try for a postponement of your trial. It is next Thursday, and the climate is just not right. If the trial comes this early, you will get 12 to 15 years. If I can obtain even a sixty day postponement, perhaps we can get it reduced to 2 to 5 years."

"No Sir, Mr. Lawyer," answered Sue. "I have turned my life over to Jesus and I want to know what He has in mind for me right now."

"I insist on a postponement," interrupted her lawyer.

"I insist on the trial going as now scheduled," Sue demanded!

Sue didn't seem to have a chance. All of the evidence was against her.

After the first day of the trial, she called me. "Coach, this is Sue. You are the first one I have called. God has performed a miracle. Even though I am guilty, God has proclaimed me not guilty, and I am a free woman tonight."

Sue had covenanted with God that when He freed her, she would serve Him, read the Bible and attend church and Bible Study.

Friends, when we covenant with God, He knows the future, and He knows if we are going to carry through with our covenant. We might think we are but He knows whether we are or not. God knew that Sue was sincere when she made her covenant with Him!

There was a lot of static about the lawyers, courts, judges, concerning Sue's release. I did not criticize them as I happen to know that they didn't have anything to do with it.

Friends, before we are too critical about my friend, Sue, let us realize that what God did for Sue is exactly the same He did for each one of us believers. *Though we are guilty He has proclaimed us not guilty, and has cleansed us through the atonement of the precious blood of Jesus on the cross!*

I am happy to report that the last time I saw Sue and her daughter, Norma, in the community in which she is now living, God is blessing them. Sue and Norma are healthy. She has a good job. Sue is reading the Bible, attending Church, attending a weekly Bible Study, and studying a discipleship course. Most of all she is bringing Norma up in the nurture and admonition of the Lord!

I praise God for my friend Sue and her strong desire to live a life pleasing to her Jesus. I praise Jesus that He fulfills every promise to Sue, and me, and all other believers who really trust in Him!

The Devil Must Have Set This Up

"Coach, I want you to look at this poster I made," Marcia said as she held it up. I read the poster.

"Come and rap with Coach Eby from Coldwater, Michigan. Monday night from 7:00 to 9:00 at the

Townhouse apartment clubhouse. All teenagers welcomed. No adults allowed!"

Two of my Christian friends, Don and Marcia had invited me out to Denver, Colorado, for meetings. I was staying at their apartment.

"No one knows who I am out here, Marcia. Do you think anyone will show?"

"I have reserved the clubhouse just for you for those two hours," Marcia answered. "I want you there. There will be no ping pong playing or pool. It is just reserved for your meeting."

"I will be there, Marcia," I promised.

At 7:00 Monday night I walked into the clubhouse. Something had gone wrong with Marcia's reservation. There were five pot smoking teenagers, two boys and three girls. They were playing pool, smoking, running around, screaming, cursing, and telling dirty stories.

I thought to myself: "God, you didn't set up this appointment. The devil must have set it up. These kids don't want to hear about the Bible and Jesus." I sat down and waited.

Shortly, three teenagers showed up to rap with Coach Eby. Two girls and one boy. The boy and his sister were brought to the clubhouse by their father. The father and mother had accepted Jesus the day before as I was knocking on doors.

I asked the three teenagers to sit down. Then I talked to my Lord. "Lord, there is no way I can talk to these three teenagers in this atmosphere. They won't even be able to hear me. The distractions are just too much. Certainly the Holy Spirit will be quenched by all this hollering, cursing, smoking, and confusion.

"Should I take these three teenagers to my friend's apartment, and talk to them about Jesus in the quietness of the apartment? If that is what you want me to do, Lord, then I am asking for a sign to indicate your will. If you don't tell me Lord, I am going to stay here. You know Lord that I sincerely believe that you send me every place I go. I cannot leave here unless you tell me to."

I sat and sat with no leading from God. The three teenagers were getting restless, and so was I. I knew something had to be done quick.

As the other group knocked the last ball into the pocket, and started racking them up again, I jumped to my feet and moved over to the pool table. I raised both of my fists above my head and shouted at the five young people.

"How many of you are going to put those pool sticks down, and come over in the corner and rap with Coach Eby from Coldwater, Michigan. What about it, right now?" I yelled.

One of the boys took his cigarette out of his mouth blew smoke at me, and sarcastically asked, "What do you think you are going to rap about anyway, Man?"

"That doesn't matter one bit," I yelled. "How many of you are going to come over right now and listen? If you don't like it, you can go back to playing pool or get out. Come right over now and listen."

All five shuffled over to the corner and sat down in chairs and placed their feet up on other chairs. They started blowing smoke rings at me. I commenced telling them about some interesting incidents that had happened to me in athletics and flying, trying to get their attention.

I had talked only about two minutes, when another teenage boy burst into the room from the outside door. I took one look at him, and I could tell right then that he was the roughest and toughest of the bunch. He didn't come to the clubhouse to rap with Coach Eby about the Bible and Jesus.

The eight other teenagers were sitting in chairs and I was standing as I talked to them. As the new kid came in the door, I immediately raced over to meet him. I grabbed him by the shoulders and shook him.

"Man are you ever lucky. You got here just in time to rap with Coach Eby from Coldwater, Michigan. I saved a special seat for you. There, you sit down and listen." I pushed him down into an empty chair."

From a commune to marriage and a
beautiful family in Jesus.

He was taken by surprise and he really didn't know what
to do. So he put his feet up on another chair and also blew
smoke at me.

I continued to talk about some humorous incidents. I then
swung into the Bible and Jesus. Right then, I thought, I was
going to lose all nine of them. While I continued talking to
them, I talked ten times as fast to my Jesus.

"Jesus, this is your department. If you want them to
knock my teeth down my throat, if you want them to go back
to playing pool, if you want them to leave, or if you want
them to listen, this is of your doing."

The more I talked, the more it was evident that Jesus and
the Holy Spirit were taking over. Forty-five minutes later, all
nine teenagers accepted Jesus and joined the Family of God.

I gave out free Bibles and books, and then closed with a
circle prayer holding hands.

I fervently asked my Jesus to bless these new children of
God and my new brothers and sisters in Christ.

After the prayer, the boy who had burst into the room,

immediately raced out of the room. In five minutes he was back with two boys. He was back of them and had hold of each one of them by the inside shoulder. He pushed them up to me.

"Coach, these are my two best buddies. They need this Jesus, also. You tell 'em."

I did.

I recorded all the names, addresses, and telephone numbers so I could follow up with letters, phone calls, and Bible Courses.

Friend, we must understand that these decisions had nothing to do with Coach Eby. Obviously, the seed had already been sewn. Perhaps by pastors, Sunday school teachers, neighbors, or friends. Prayer had been sent to an all-loving, compassionate God, concerning all of these teenagers. I just happened to be around when our Lord gave the increase. Praise God from whom all blessings flow!

Does This Mean I Have To Give Up My Dope?

John, a college student, was hooked on hard dope. When he was discovered by college authorities, they thought he might die.

John was sent to a hospital. Fortunately he survived, and a week later was discharged and sent back to college. John called his parents who were Christians. He told them what had happened. Of course, they were heartbroken. I didn't know the family at the time.

"Mom and Dad, I have a real problem and I don't know what to do. I am scared to think what might happen to me. I heard a fellow by the name of Coach Eby speak up north some time back. I believe that he could help me with my dope problem."

John's parents made the long trip to the college and brought John to my house on a Sunday afternoon. Although I had not been notified, God is good and is still performing miracles. God had me home that Sunday afternoon for a few

From drugs to Jesus.

hours.

As I invited the three in, John introduced himself. "Coach Eby, I believe you can help me with my dope problem."

"John," I answered, "Let us go down in my basement recreation room. We will leave your folks up here to talk with my wife."

Downstairs, I said to him, "John, I can't really help you with your dope problem, but Jesus can. With your permission I would like to tell you about Jesus."

John was willing and thirty-five minutes later accepted Jesus.

"Coach, does this mean I have to give up my dope?"

"You don't have to give up anything, John."

"What did you say Coach?"

"I said you don't have to give up anything," I shouted.

"What kind of church do you go to, Coach?"

"I am not talking about church, John. I am talking about God's Plan for our lives."

"What do you mean, Coach?" John asked.

"I will tell you what I mean, John. I know something about you, and you know the same thing about me. You are too weak to give up dope. You and I are too weak to run our own lives. We will not, and can not, give up things --- because we are too weak. But God is strong, John. As children of God we can rely upon the Lord's strength.

"God only asks us to do one thing. That is to be His close friend. As we discipline ourselves to do the things necessary to become His close friend, God will control our lives through the Holy Spirit. He will change our lives, and take things away from us and make it a blessing. We don't give it up. He just takes dope and other things away from us at the accepted time."

I received a couple of letters from John after he went back to college. Three weeks later, he hitch-hiked to my house, and flew to West Virginia for a two-day youth retreat. During a quiet time, John stood up and gave his testimony. I praise God for His strength and His ability to change any of our lives if we will only completely surrender to Him!

Do You Know Why You Are Here?

I was visiting a couple of my friends in an adjacent county. The lady had been released from the hospital, and was confined to her bed at home. After visiting with her for a few minutes and praying with her, she interrupted me.

"Coach, do you know why you are here?"

"Certainly," I answered. "I am here to visit you, my sister in Christ."

"No you're not," she insisted. "You are here so I can tell you how to drive over to Dan's and tell him about Jesus. You see, Coach, Dan is dying of cancer and he doesn't know Jesus. I believe you were sent over here so I could send you there."

After receiving instructions on how to drive to Dan's place, I jumped in my car and started off. On the way home I had planned to stop at an evangelistic meeting at a nearby town. I did not have any responsibility to the meeting but wanted to visit and observe the working of our Lord.

As I approached Dan's place, I passed a young boy and

girl walking along the road. I stopped and asked them if they knew where Dan lived?

The boy spoke up. "Right down at the next house, mister, but he is not at home. He went over to his in-laws."

"When do you expect that he might be home?" I inquired.

The young fellow chirped right back, "Well you never can tell. You know Dan and his wife get over to their relatives, and they will eat and talk and talk." I thanked the boy and girl for the information.

I drove six more miles to the evangelistic meeting. As the meeting came near the end, I had made up my mind that I would go on home rather than backtrack twelve miles to see Dan. I rationalized that he wouldn't be home yet anyway. No use wasting the time. Anyway, the baseball playoffs were on television.

However, as the meeting ended, I was asked to counsel with a couple, which I did. When I was through, I decided it was now too late to visit Dan as he would be home and in bed. I would still have time to see the last three innings of the baseball game.

As I drove my car toward home, it made a left turn instead of going straight. I found myself heading toward Dan's house. I did not know Dan or his family. There was a light in the house. I pulled into the driveway, approached the house and knocked on the door. I could see through the door. A young man was on the telephone. I assumed it was Dan. I could hear him through the screen door.

Dan looked at me through the doorway, and I could hear him say, "I have to hang up now. Coach Eby is here."

My dear sister in Christ had called him and let him know I was coming. It also turned out that I had Dan's wife in school as one of my students.

Dan, his wife, Jill, and a teenage neighbor girl and I sat down around the kitchen table. With their permission, we opened up the Word of God. I explained God's wonderful plan for our lives and our future. All three accepted Jesus and joined the Family of God!

I gave all of them Bibles and books, and followed up in the usual way with letters and Bible Courses. Dan started reading the Word of God and growing spiritually. As he became worse physically, he became stronger spiritually.

I visited Dan in the hospital, and was thrilled to see how his faith had increased. He improved somewhat physically and came back home where I visited him a couple more times.

Just recently God has seen fit to take Dan home to his rewards. Praise the Lord that we believers like Dan have the future guaranteed.

Do You Really Know Jesus?

I was speaking to a thousand women at a women's weekend retreat. I closed one of my messages with a testimony about a young mother who had tortured her 18 month old daughter until she died. Later on in the jail, I was able to talk with this mother and see her accept Christ.

Immediately after the message, two ladies approached me and asked if they could talk to me. I took them over to a private table, and we all three sat down around the table. Their names were Kelly and Jenny.

"Coach, how could anyone that committed such a crime to an innocent child be accepted by God, and be forgiven by God?" Kelly wanted to know.

Jenny spoke up, "What would happen to the baby in a case like that?"

"Kelly, do you really know Jesus as your personal Saviour?" I asked. "Have you really had a personal encounter with Jesus Christ? Is He really a vital part of your life?"

Tears appeared in Kelly's eyes as she said no.

"What about you, Jenny?" She shook her head no.

It was only a short time later, as we went through the Word of God, that we all got right with God. We might not understand why God allows such things to happen, but if we know Jesus in a personal and intimate way, we will accept His sovereignty and power to forgive and take care of any situation as we put our complete trust in Him!

Although I live a long ways from Kelly, Jenny, and their families, God has been so good to allow me to have fellowship and worship with them several times. These two sisters in Christ and their families mean so much to me as we have shared together the blessings of God!

God Doesn't Answer Prayers That Quickly

I received the following letter from Jackson Prison: "Dear Coach Eby, my name is Mickey. As I was put back into my cell the other day, I laid down on my bunk. As my eyes gazed around the cell, I saw a book on the floor. I got up out of my bunk, and went over and picked it up. Laying back down on my bunk, I started reading it. It was the book you wrote, 'Calling God's Tower, Come In Please.'

"I read a couple of pages and decided that stuff wasn't for me. I threw the book across the cell and against the opposite wall. It bounced and fell on the floor. A few minutes later, I looked back at the book and the pages were turning. I said to myself, 'I wish that stupid book would shut up.' The pages stopped turning, and the book remained open. Once again I got out of my bunk and picked up the book. It was opened to Chapter 3, and I read Chapter 3. It made sense to me and I took the three steps in belief through faith and accepted Jesus. I read more of the book especially Chapter 4 about the need of getting close to God. Then I picked up a Bible in the cell and commenced reading it. This all happened Saturday afternoon and evening.

"I then started praying that God would send you up here so I and some other fellows could talk to you. That night I had a dream that you were coming up to the prison to speak to us.

"The next morning on Sunday I decided that I was going to Chapel Services with my buddy who had been trying to get

From unbelievers to one Family in Christ.

me to go for months. I had always refused. My buddy was real surprised when I told him I was going with him from now on. I had informed him that I was now a Christian. I told him about your book, and the dream I had.

"My buddy told me not to take much stock in dreams, and that Coach Eby would never come up to the prison. He would be too busy to bother with us inmates."

This happened to be the Sunday that the prison Chaplain had scheduled Coach Eby to come to speak at Chapel Services.

I spoke at an eight o'clock service, then proceeded to go inside the walls to speak at the nine o'clock service.

By the time the Chaplain and I arrived at the second service, about 400 inmates and the choir were singing hymns. As we walked down the aisle to the speaker's platform, Mickey stood up and pointed at me and shouted to his buddy.

"I told you he would be here! That is Coach Eby! I recognized him from his picture. That is him. I told you so. I told you so!"

"Sit down you nut," his buddy answered. "That can't be

him. It just looks like him. Anyways, God doesn't answer prayers that quick."

As I walked down the aisle, I wondered why that inmate was standing up and pointing at me. The Chaplain soon introduced me as Coach Eby from Coldwater, Michigan.

Mickey jumped up again and shouted to his buddy, "I told you so. I told you so!"

After the service I was able to spend a few minutes with Mickey and some of the others. It was thrilling to see our Lord work among lives even behind bars and walls. As I was speaking, I could see many radiant faces of inmates who undoubtedly loved Jesus.

The Power Of Prayer

"Coach Eby, this is Vern. I understand that eight months from now you are scheduled to have meetings in the Columbus, Ohio, area on Friday, Saturday, and Sunday. Is that right?" I told him to hold the phone while I checked my calendar. I then confirmed the dates.

Vern continued. "We want to have you reserve the entire week for that area."

"What for, Vern?"

"We are going to pray you into the public schools of the area, Coach."

"Vern, do you realize what I talk about no matter where I go? I talk about the Bible and Jesus."

"We know that," he answered. "That is what we want. That is the reason we are going to pray you in."

"Well, you will have to, Vern, because I won't. I want to be sure it is God's Will and not my own desire. If God doesn't prepare the way, we will be in trouble."

"The way we look at it, Coach, God will not allow you to go in unless He has prepared the way."

"I'll buy that, Vern. I will reserve the week to see how our Lord reacts to your prayers."

A week before the meetings, Vern called me and told me

that they had prayed me into 12 public school assemblies for 30 to 40 minutes to talk to the student bodies about the Bible and Jesus. I am firmly convinced that Vern and his wife, and many friends and wives, spent hours praying to our Loving Saviour for these meetings. The results proved it!

All of the school administrators cordially welcomed us. The students were attentive, courteous, and receptive. Over three thousand students went out of their way to voluntarily pick up a copy of the Christian book, "Calling God's Tower, Come in Please." There was no static during or after the meetings.

God states in *James 5:16a* "*The effectual fervent prayer of a righteous man availeth much.*"

This Family found real help and happiness through the Bible and Jesus.

"O taste and see that the Lord is good:
blessed is the man that trusteth in Him."
Psalm 34:8

9

PRAISE THE LORD

"Without Me, Ye Can Do Nothing"

The principal of a southern public high school contacted me. "Coach Eby, you don't know me and I don't know you. I have read your book and would like to have you come down and speak to our entire student body."

"Mr Hamilton, what can I say in my message?"

"Coach, you can say anything that you printed in your book."

"I will be there Mr. Hamilton."

The date was set for Thursday, February 19, which was about six months away. As I traveled and spoke at Christian meetings, I asked people to pray for February 19; to pray that something great was going to happen in a southern public high school. Not because of me, but because of a wonderful, compassionate, all powerful God that had opened the doors, and would answer the prayers of His people concerning this opportunity.

After being bathed in prayer by thousands of Christians for a period of months, the day arrived. I planned on a day of traveling. Then God changed my mode of transportation. I was unable to fly my plane because of forecast tornados.

I left Coldwater on Wednesday morning at 4:30. Fourteen hours later I drove into town. I located a church and went to a prayer meeting where I enlisted more prayer support for the next day's meeting. I then checked into a motel for the night.

I covenanted with God that I was going to bed at exactly 11:00 p.m. and sleep until 6:00 a.m. With seven hours of wonderful sleep, I would be raring to go when I spoke at the assembly. As planned, I went to bed at eleven, but I was so excited that I couldn't sleep. All I could do was to think about the opportunity to tell these young boys and girls about my Jesus.

I rolled and tossed, and tossed and rolled for hours.

Finally, I couldn't stand it any longer. I rolled out of bed and got on my knees at the bed side. I prayed for awhile. I then stood up, and went to the buffet, and looked at my watch. It was 4:00 a.m.

I picked up the Bible off the buffet, and it opened to John Chapter 15. I started reading until I reached the fifth verse where I read. "And Eby without me, ye can do nothing."

"Yea, Lord, that I know." I picked up the phone and called a pastor friend of mine in that area. At least he used to be my friend, until I called him at 4:00 a.m.

"Pastor Jim, this is Coach Eby. Do you know about the assembly we are having in the high school this morning?"

"Floyd, you know that I know about that assembly!"

"OK Pastor, then get up and read the Gospel of John, Chapter 15 Verse 5 and start praying." I then hung up.

I arrived at the school early and greeted the teachers, administrators, coaches, and many of the students as they came in. I located the principal in his office. "Mr. Hamilton, I understand that the assembly is at 9:00 a.m.

How much time am I allowed?"

"Coach Eby, you can have all the time you need."

I could hardly believe my ears. God does answer prayers.

"Mr. Hamilton, if God doesn't have their attention, I will quit in five minutes, but if He has their attention, I will go forty minutes." Mr. Hamilton concurred.

The assembly was held in the gymnasium. Speaking conditions were bad. I stood at one end of the gym with students on both sides in the bleachers and no one in front of me. The PA system was inadequate so I did not use it. I had to swing my gaze back and forth across the gym to make eye contact with the students. Most of them were too far away to make contact. Acoustics were bad. I had to almost shout to be heard.

"Lord, I thought, "Nothing profitable can come of this assembly except as of you. I commit it entirely to you including all of the problems I am facing." I thought of *Luke 1:37 For with God nothing shall be impossible.*

I spoke for forty minutes and closed the message with this suggestion: "Students if God has been speaking to you this morning, and you want to get right with God, I invite you to come to the driver education room in the basement of the next building. You may come by yourself, or with a friend, or in small groups. We will open up the Bible and read the verses and take the steps that Coach Eby took overseas to become a Child of God." I closed with a short prayer.

I stayed for two days as 230 high school boys and girls came in to see me to get right with God. I gave away 230 books, "Calling God's Tower, Come in Please," and also 460 Bibles, two to each student who talked with me.

After I arrived home, I wrote 230 letters, one to each student. I am still receiving letters and making contacts with my brothers and sisters in Christ. I was invited, a year later, to talk to the Junior High school students.

I praise God for Christian administrators and teachers who recognize the real need in the public schools. God really does answer prayers, and He is unlimited!

PRAISE THE LORD/153

Saved as a result of a snow storm.

Turned On By Teenagers

As I was flying home from a morning worship service, I was scheduled to stop on the way at a church youth group meeting in a home. I landed at the airport, and the youth leaders picked me up. The meeting was at their home.

I spoke to about 25 teenagers as they sat around on the floor and in chairs. I ended the message with a testimony showing how short the time is, even with teenagers. After the testimony, I gave an invitation.

"If God has been speaking to you, who is the first one that is willing to go back into the family room with Coach Eby and get right with God."

One little tenth grade girl raised her hand, and started toward me. "I want to go with you Coach."

"Great, come with me," I answered. I grabbed her hand and led her out into the family room. We both sat down in chairs.

Before we could start talking, eleven more teenagers came into the family room and sat down. All thirteen of us discussed God's Plan for our lives. We all became brothers and sisters in Christ and twelve teenagers joined the Family of God.

After closing with a circle prayer asking God's blessings upon my new found friends and brothers and sisters in Christ, I gathered the necessary information I needed for followup, including names, addresses, and phone numbers.

I decided it was time to fly home. I made my way through the living room where there were some teenagers who had not come back with the group. Before I could get to the door to leave for the airport, another tenth grade girl came up to me and grabbed my hand, and sort of whimpered. "Coach Eby, will you still talk with people in the family room?"

"Sure, Sally, come with me. I have lots of time."

As Sally and I made our way back to the family room, five more teenagers followed us and I ended up with six more brothers and sisters in Christ. I finally reached the airport, but to tell you truthfully, friends, I didn't need my plane. I was so turned on after eighteen teenagers got right with God, that I could have flown home without my plane. I was already up in the clouds.

About three weeks later I was due to fly past the same city on my way to weekend meetings. I called the sponsors of the youth group.

"If you will have my brothers and sisters come to the airport at 11:00 a.m. this Saturday, I will give them all free airplane rides." The youth group was there in full force.

After the airplane rides, we all had sack lunches. They brought one for Coach Eby, also. After lunch with the permission of the airport manager, we all went into the terminal building and sat down on the floor in a circle. I opened up the Word and we had a sweet hour of fellowship with each other and our Lord.

After closing in prayer, I flew out for my next commitment with everyone waving goodbye as I flew over the airport, tilting my wings to my friends. Before I was out of sight, I was already homesick to see them again. I praise God for teenagers. When they get right with God, they are really used of God!

They Are Too Young Coach

Jack and Jane were attending my midnight Bible Study on Wednesday nights. Both of them had accepted Jesus and were "on fire" for Him!

One night after the study, they stopped me out in the street. "Coach, we wish you would call upon our folks and tell them about Jesus," Jack said.

"I will, Jack and Jane, if you get their permission to have me do so. You know that I never talk to people about Jesus unless they want me to."

Both Jack and Jane were seventeen and seniors in high school. They were engaged and planned on being married the summer after graduation. They wanted me to marry them.

After much prayer by Jack and Jane, arrangements had been made for the four parents to meet me at my house on a certain Sunday afternoon. During this meeting I told the parents how God had changed my life and how He had changed Jack's and Jane's lives. All four parents professed the Lord.

Before they left the parents wanted to talk with me about the forthcoming marriage.

"Coach, every one of us love Jack and Jane. We have nothing against them marrying each other, but they are just too young. Do you realize they are only seventeen? What do you think about it? You are marrying them."

"Friends, let me tell you something," I said. "Jack and Jane really love the Lord Jesus. It is real with them. When I marry them, they will be one in Christ. I would rather marry Jack and Jane at seventeen when they are one in Christ, than to marry them at the age of forty without Christ. I have no doubt about the success of this marriage. I believe Jack and Jane will stay on God's program for their lives."

The reason I was so sure of the success of this marriage

was that I had seen Jack and Jane in action in the Lord's service. Nearly every Thursday night, even before their marriage, Jack would go to the jail to speak to the inmates. He told them how he had been in trouble with the law, and with dope, and how he had had a messy life. When he turned his life over to Jesus, he told them, our Lord had really blessed him. He told the inmates how they could find the same joy that he had found.

While Jack was talking to the inmates, Jane was downstairs or out in the car praying for Jack and the inmates. Both Jack and Jane have taken a special course in jail ministry to qualify them to hold services in jails. Both of them continue to be active in their Church and active in serving Jesus through personal witnessing.

The 700 Club

I was invited to be on The 700 Club television program out of Portsmouth, Virginia. After confirming the date, they sent me a list of instructions. I really appreciate the consideration they gave me. I was not asked about my church or doctrine.

From my background and my book, they knew I loved the Lord Jesus, and this seemed good enough for them. I agreed whole heartily with all of their suggestions. The instructions included the suggestion that I not knock any particular denomination, movement, or individual Christian.

As they said, "We are not here to offend people but to win and help them." Praise the Lord. This is my feeling also.

Because of convenience I flew my own plane to Virginia after a Sunday morning service in Kentucky. I arrived in Norfolk, Virginia, in time to check into a motel, and attend an evening service in a nearby church.

After much prayer and Bible reading, God gave me a good night's rest. The next morning I took a taxi to the studio arriving an hour before program time. This gave me the opportunity to get acquainted with the band members, program directors, makeup girls, camera men and program interviewers. This is a wonderful group of people who really love the Lord.

The studio crew left nothing undone to make me feel at home. They helped me become familiar with the studio, the program format, and each detail that concerned my participation. Even though every one was busy, someone would stop and pray with me, asking God's blessing upon me and the program.

The program director instructed me to watch the first part of the program on the monitor in a small room. At a certain point in the program I was to leave the room and come to a specific corner. I was to watch the program director across the room. When he motioned to me I was to walk across the studio and shake hands with Pat and John, the two interviewers, and then sit down in a chair and Pat would take over.

The program director informed me that if everything went right I would be on about 25 minutes. He didn't have to tell me that if I bombed, I would be cut. I knew that already.

I did not have any fear. I had been on television before and realized that it was much different, talking to an interviewer, cameras, and hot flood lights than to a live audience that you could watch and note the reactions. I was all prayed up and felt ready to serve my Jesus!

Before I came on, Pat and John started discussing their next guest, Coach Eby. They talked about my flying and many varied activities surrounding it with some humor about some of my flying escapades as described in my book.

After shaking hands with Pat and John, I sat down in the middle chair. Pat started making comments and asking questions. Pat was trying to build me up about my athletic accomplishments, and I was trying to tear myself down.

"Coach Eby," Pat commented, "You must have had a real influence with your athletes according to the way these members of this state championship team turned out."

"I really didn't Pat. I am sure the Lord affected many of

their lives, and I am proud of them."

"Did you really devise the one-handed jump shot in basketball, Coach?"

"I guess we were the first ones to use it, but it wasn't because of any intelligence I might have had. It was because I had a player who couldn't play defense. We therefore went into a racehorse game, and we couldn't shoot the two-handed set shot on the run. I just told them to jump up into the air and throw the ball at the hoop as they were running."

"Well, Coach, what about inventing the split-T offense in football? Nearly everyone uses that now. How did you hit upon that?"

"Once again, Pat, it wasn't because of my genius, but because of some slow backs that couldn't run the ends. I decided that we would have to split the opponents' defense. I spread my offense across the field to make some inside holes for my slow backs."

Pat kept me in the athletic vein for some time. I was anxious to get into testimonies where Jesus had changed lives, but Pat knew what he was doing. After the program I received hundreds of letters from people with athletic interests who wanted to know about Jesus.

It seems like we had been discussing testimonies for only a few minutes when Pat stood up and shook my hand and thanked me for coming. Immediately, a thought crossed my mind, Eby, you really bombed. They only left you on for eight minutes. I couldn't understand as I thought everything seemed to be going good. Both Pat and John had seemed pleased with the interview. John had already left the stage and embraced me as I came off. He congratulated me on the interview. Program directors, band members, and some of the audience did the same.

I was somewhat confused. All of these people seemed so spiritual. Were they all hypocrites?

If I bombed, why didn't they say so and let it go at that? I was convinced that I must have bombed out or I would have been on for the full 25 minutes.

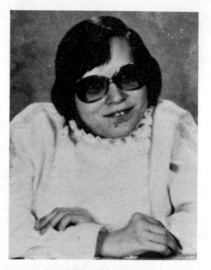

**A crippled child of God who will
soon have a perfect body.**

I didn't blame anyone except myself. I was really
perturbed with myself. Not because of me, but because my
Saviour had opened up a great opportunity, and I had failed
Him!

The program had been on live for the immediate area and
video taped for other areas to be played back later. I was so
concerned with myself flubbing the opportunity that I didn't
even stay to watch it played back. I immediately went to the
airport and flew my plane back home.

The program was to be on television a week later in our
area. Friends in my home town asked me, "How did the
national television program go, Coach?"

"Terrible," I answered. "If it is as bad as I think, I will be
leaving town after Monday night."

As my wife and I watched the program on Monday night
by ourselves, I found out that I actually was on for 27
minutes. I had been so interested during the program that I
had lost all track of time. I could also see that the Lord had
touched hearts during the program. The people in the studio

had been sincere in saying that God had blessed the program.

Hundreds of letters indicated that God, not me, had been in control. Praise His Holy Name! Dear Lord please be sure that I walk through all doors that you open, and that each one will only glorify you!

Coach Get Your Own Relationship Right With Jesus

As I was having a couple of weeks meetings in Florida, a Pastor drove me to Alabama one night to give the devotions to a group of teenagers who were at a roller skating party. We stopped at the church where the youth group would come after the party. At the church, the youth were to have their devotions, games, and pizza.

I asked the two Pastors if we could have devotions in the sanctuary as soon as the bus brought the youth back from the rink. The teenagers could then go to the fellowship hall for games and pizza. I felt the sanctuary would be a better environment for the Holy Spirit to work after the active skating. The Pastors agreed.

As I spoke, I could see that God was talking to many young people and I closed with this invitation. "If God has been speaking to you tonight, and you want to get right with God, as we go to the fellowship hall, come to me in the corner. We will get right with God before we play games and eat pizza."

I went back to a corner of the hall, and two teenage girls sidled up to me without saying a word.

"Would you two gals like to rap with Coach Eby?"

"Yeh," they answered.

I pulled up a couple of chairs and asked them to sit down. I sat down in a chair facing them. As I sat down, fourteen more boys and girls came and sat down in chairs. I went through the salvation scriptures discussing the meaning of each. God really had the attention of each one. All sixteen were listening intently. They were not paying any attention to the distraction of noisy games and the smell of pizza. Thirty minutes later, all sixteen of them professed Jesus, and joined the Family of God!

While I was talking to the group, the Pastor of the Church told my Pastor friend who brought me, "Why don't you tell that friend of yours to break that meeting up, the pizza is getting cold."

My Pastor friend answered, "No way. Don't you see how God has their attention? Not one of them is paying any attention to these games or the pizza. They are getting right with God."

The sixteen teenagers and I closed our discussion holding hands in a circle prayer. The group went and got their pizza and then came back to talk some more about Jesus.

On the way back to Florida that night, my pastor friend told me what the other pastor had said about breaking up the discussion about Jesus because the pizza was getting cold.

My first reaction was a carnal one. I thought, "What's the matter with that guy. Here he is, a minister, a man of God, and he is worried about the pizza getting cold! He should be praising God because some youth of his church came into the Family of God." My thoughts were giving me bad feelings about that pastor.

"Forgive me, Jesus, for thinking bad about that pastor. I know he loves you, Lord, and I know he wants his youth to be right with you. I love him, Lord. Please forgive me my sin of judging. Please help me to get my own relationship back with you where it should be. I have all I can do to keep my relationship right with You without being critical about someone else.

"I love you, Lord, and I love that pastor. Whatever he said is between You and him. It has nothing to do with me. Remember Lord, you took my inspection badge away from me three years ago. You told me that you wanted me to stay out of that department; that You would take charge of the judging department. Thank you Jesus for setting me straight once again!"

The next day the pastor called long distance to apologize for his actions. I don't believe he would have, though, if I had not straightened out my own relationship with Jesus on this matter. I am not to judge people. As I keep my relationship right with Jesus, He will take care of everyone else. Praise God for such a Holy and just Saviour!

One In Christ

"Coach Eby, my husband has left me and the children. I just don't know what to do. Would you come over?"

Irma was crying. I didn't know her, but apparently she knew about me. Irma accepted the new way of life in Jesus.

"Now Irma," I encouraged her, "You can now have a wonderful, happy, fruitful life in Jesus with or without your husband. If you will just follow God's Program for your life."

Irma started attending a weekly Bible Study and church and Sunday school. She brought her two girls with her. She also started reading the Bible, talking with God, being with other Christians, and serving Jesus.

God started blessing her and changing her life. No longer did Irma cry about her husband, she just turned him over to the Lord. However, he divorced Irma and married another woman.

Six months later Irma introduced me to a friend. Larry was also divorced and had the custody of his two sons. I invited Larry and Irma to a crusade meeting. After the service, Larry drove all the way home and then called me on the phone.

"Coach Eby, could I see you tomorrow night after work?"

God had already touched Larry's heart and he accepted Jesus the next night.

Six months later, I had the privilege of performing the marriage ceremony as Larry and Irma were united one in Christ. What a beautiful Christian Family. Mom and Dad, two daughters, and two sons. Larry and Irma are bringing their children up in the nurture and admonition of the Lord.

They are also setting the example for their children. Mom and Dad continue to discipline themselves to follow God's spiritual program including taking a disciple course to tell others about Jesus. I praise God for their dedication and their love for Jesus!

A ninth grade girl gets right with God and is used of God to bring her entire family to Jesus.

*"You are living a brand new kind of life
that is continually learning more and more
of what is right, and trying constantly to
be more and more like Christ who created
this new life within you."*
Colossians 3:10

10

THINGS ARE DIFFERENT NOW

Listen Mister I Want Practical Advice

The phone rang. "Coach Eby, this is Bonnie Smith. You don't know me and I don't know you. I understand that you talk with people who have problems. Is that right?"

"I do, Bonnie, only if God opens the doors. Only God solves problems."

"Would you come over?" Bonnie asked.

I agreed and followed her instructions on how to get to her house. Bonnie opened the door, invited me in, and asked me to sit down.

She immediately took off on me. "Coach Eby, I want you to know that my husband left me three weeks ago. He is living with another women and has left me alone with our three children. I called you over here for only one purpose. To tell me how I can change my husband."

"That is simple, Bonnie. You can't. But you can change your own relationship with God."

"I want you to know Coach Eby that I am a Christian but he isn't."

"That is fine, Bonnie. Since you are a child of God, then you certainly can change your relationship with Him."

"I want you to know, sir," Bonnie interrupted, "I am not the one that needs changing. My husband is the one that needs to be changed."

"That might well be, Bonnie, but you still can't change your husband. But you can bring your own relationship with Jesus to the point that He will help you." I started telling Bonnie how she could do this.

She interrupted again. "I have you pegged already, Mr. Eby. You are one of those dreamy Christians way up in the clouds who never has anything bad happen to them. Therefore you are always going around Praising the Lord. I am not that kind of a woman or Christian. I am a practical woman and a practical Christian. Mister, I want some practical advice!"

"Oh, you want to be practical, is that right, Bonnie?"

"That's right," she answered.

"Well, let's be practical Bonnie. I want you to know that I travel all over the United States and Canada telling people about this New Way of Life. I am not on anybody's payroll. I pay my own expense.

"As I fly these long distances and travel many hours in my car and plane, I get weary and exhausted and sometimes sick. Many times I wish I were home where I have the comforts of life, and be with my own family.

"Instead of being here with you tonight, I could be home sitting in my easy chair drinking lemonade, eating ice cream, and watching the ball game on TV. Do you think I am dumb enough to travel all over the United States without pay and be here tonight to tell you about something that doesn't work?

"I know it works. It has worked in my own life and in the lives of thousands of other people I have worked with. I ask you again, Bonnie, do you really think I am that dumb?"

Bonnie answered softly, "That does sound practical. That does make sense."

"You bet it does," I said.

"I'll buy that, Coach. What do I do for my husband?"

"Pray for him," I answered.

"That will be mighty, mighty, mighty difficult. But I will try," Bonnie consented. "But what will I do about that woman?"

"Pray for her also," I suggested.

"Never, never, never, no never," she exclaimed.

"Bonnie, when you can pray for that husband and the woman he is living with without malice in your heart, you will have changed your relationship with Jesus to such an extent that you will have a happy life with or without that man."

"OK, Coach, I will try. How should I go about it."

"It is simple, Bonnie, but it takes discipline. I asked you to go on the following spiritual program: Daily Bible Reading, talking with God many times each day, be with other Christians as much as possible, weekly attendance at all the church services and a weekly Bible study, and serve Jesus when He shows you what to do. If you are not praising God within sixty days, you can forget it."

Bonnie really went on the program. While many start the program and soon drop it, Bonnie stuck to it. She was praising God in two weeks.

One day, Bonnie came to me. "Coach, I still love my husband. I wish he were back home with me and the children. However, I have turned him over to Jesus. The other day I was driving downtown and I saw him coming out of the bakery. I took my left hand off the steering wheel and pointed my finger at him and shouted, "There he is, God. You can have him! If you want him to come back home, you will have to take him into your family. That's the only way it would be right!" God blessed Bonnie for putting her trust completely in Him!

One day I received a call from a hospital in a nearby city. It was Bonnie and she was crying. "Coach Eby, I never ask you to do too much for me, do I?"

"Wait a minute, Bonnie, let us get something straight. You're my sister in Christ. I love you and I am concerned for you. What do you want?"

"Coach, my father is eighty years old and is dying of cancer here in the hospital. Two doctors came in this morning and told him that he would die today or tomorrow. He could not live beyond tomorrow. Coach, he doesn't know Jesus. I have been trying to tell him like you told me to. Every time I talk to him I start to cry. I just can't do it. I asked him if I could invite Coach Eby over and he said yes. Coach, I know how busy you are, but would you come over to talk to my father?"

There are times when we must let the Lord set our priorities. I picked up my pen off the desk, and marked a great big cross across my afternoon appointments. "Bonnie, you have some one pick me up at the airport in an hour."

As I flew to the airport I prayed that my Lord would show me the correct approach to tell an eighty year old man dying of cancer about Jesus. God just didn't give me the answer.

Bonnie's mother picked me up at the airport. I continued to pray for the right approach as we drove to the hospital. We took the elevator and then walked down the hall to the room, but still no answer from God.

The room was filled with relatives and friends from all over the United States. They knew that their father, father-in-law, uncle, cousin or friend was going to die by tomorrow.

God is good. He cleared the room of everyone except Bonnie's father. I walked into the room, just me and the Holy Spirit.

I wanted to check and see if his mind was clear. "Steve, do you know me?" I shook his hand.

"Yes," he answered. "I met you once. Also Bonnie has told me all about you."

Right then God gave me His answer on the approach to be used. "Steve, when I get through talking to you, I have to fly

Jesus brought this family happiness.

my plane to Clare to speak tonight. Do you know where that
is?''

"Sure," he answered. "I had a business at Ithaca for
years." I knew his mind was clear.

"Do you know, Steve, that as I fly my plane to Clare
tonight, I could crash and be dead before you are?"

"Yes, Coach, I realize that is possible."

"Doesn't it make sense, Steve, that you and I open up the
Bible and both get right with God before something happens
to either one of us?"

"Yes, Coach, that makes sense."

I opened up God's Word and read the salvation verses to
my friend, Steve. I told him about God's wonderful plan for
my life and his life. We discussed the three steps it takes to
have an encounter with Jesus.

In forty minutes, Steve accepted Jesus and joined the
Family of God, and passed from death unto life. I took his
hand and prayed. I praised and thanked God for coming
into our lives.

I went out in the hall and announced to the friends and relatives. "Brother Steve is now in the Hands of our Heavenly Father, and is right with God. We need to be no longer concerned about Steve's future." According to Bonnie, several of her relatives were not Christians.

After flying to Clare and speaking, I arrived back at my home airport about midnight. Because I was not sure how long our Lord would keep Steve around here, I wrote my new brother a letter before I went to bed.

Steve didn't die that day, or the next day. God left him here for thirty days. According to Bonnie, Steve talked to the nurses and doctors, friend and relatives for the 30 days.

He told them how he had accepted Jesus, and how they also ought to accept Him before something happened to them. My brother, Steve, probably did more witnessing in his last 30 days than many Christians do in a lifetime.

At the end of thirty days, the Lord took him home to his rewards. I was unable to go to the funeral but visited the funeral home the night before.

After the funeral Bonnie came to me. "Coach, this is the little brown testament you gave my father. My mother said I could keep it. I want you to look in the back of it."

I did, and read, "MY DECISION TO RECEIVE CHRIST AS MY SAVIOUR. Confessing to God that I am a sinner, and believing that the Lord Jesus Christ died for my sins on the cross and was raised for my justification, I do now receive and confess Him as my personal Saviour." Underneath the above statement was the signature of Brother Steve and the date it happened. Oh, what a wonderful God we have!

Getting On The Right Track

I had an old Totor truck that I decided to sell for junk. I noticed an ad in the Shoppers' Guide wanting to buy junk cars and trucks. I called the number.

"This is Coach Eby, and I noticed your ad about buying junk trucks. I have one to sell."

"Hi, Coach Eby, this is Melvin. You called me about that old junk truck several months ago. I took a look at it and tried to call you. The line was busy, and I forgot all about it." Although I didn't know Melvin, he knew me. He had played athletics for a neighboring town.

"How much will you give me for it, Melvin?"

"Well, you know Coach, these old trucks are really not worth much."

"That's not what I asked you, Melvin. I asked you how much you would give me for it."

"Really, Coach, you can't do much with trucks like that."

"Come on, Melvin, I want to know what you will pay for that old worthless truck."

"I will give you forty or forty-five dollars," he finally committed.

"Make it fifty, Melvin, and you can have it." Although I had been a Christian for a long time, it was hard for me to lose that business streak.

"I guess, Coach, I can give you that much," but he started crying.

I thought to myself, "What is going on here, anyway? In this day of inflation would a grown man cry over five dollars?"

"Coach, my wife has left me and our children and family are split. I have wanted to talk to you. Would you take the time?"

Melvin and I set up a date to meet. Melvin had been saved two years before, but as he put it, he never got on the right track.

I gave Melvin a spiritual program to follow. Now he is on the right track. He follows the program faithfully and is now happy in Jesus!

Tears For Jesus

I was making some calls on Saturday afternoon as part of a Florida crusade. The local Pastor had given me some names and addresses of teenagers in the area. I was trying to stir up some activity for the youth rally at the church that night.

One of the calls was out in the country. This family of teenagers came to Sunday school occasionally, but never at any other time or service. The parents were not interested and never came.

I parked the car in the driveway and many of the six teenagers were out in the yard. I introduced myself to each one as the ones still in the house came out to see what was going on. After becoming acquainted with each one, I invited them to the youth rally that night at the church.

"Oh Coach, we can't come tonight."

"Why not?" I asked.

"Because we are all going fishing tonight. Dad and Mom and we have planned this for weeks. We will come in the morning to Sunday school on the church bus."

I told them I would be waiting to see them.

As the bus pulled into the church yard the next morning, I was there to greet each one. I invited them into my special Sunday school class with twenty other teenagers. With the Bible, I showed the entire class how to accept Jesus. I didn't have time to ask for individual decisions.

After I had completed the morning worship service message, I simply announced that the altar was open. I walked to the back of the church to greet the people as they left the sanctuary. Several people went to the left side of the altar and talked with God on their knees.

Then I noticed that Lilly, a thirteen year old girl from that teenage family, had slipped out of her seat. She went to her knees all by herself on the right side of the altar.

I immediately went to her and knelt beside her. Lilly was crying her eyes out for Jesus. I put my arm around her. "Lilly, do you really believe those verses and steps that we went through during Sunday school class? Do you really accept them into your being by faith in truth?"

"Oh yes, Coach, I already have. That is why I am so

happy."

"Lilly, would you like to come to our final service tonight at the church?"

"I have to come Coach. I just have to come."

"OK Lilly, I will personally pick you up tonight at your house." I knew her folks would not bring her. Lilly and I left the altar hand in hand. I picked Lilly up that night at her house. She didn't come alone. She brought her five teenage brothers and sisters. That night Lilly led all five of them to the altar and into a separate room where I could speak to them. All five of the brothers and sisters joined Lilly in the Family of God that night. I sincerely believe that these teenagers will be the means through which their parents will come to Jesus.

From Germany to a confrontation with God in their own home and acceptance of Jesus.

What Kind Of A God Do We Have, Anyway?

Ed called me on the phone. "Coach, what kind of a God do we have anyway?"

I could tell immediately that Ed was mad at me and God. "What's the matter, Ed?"

"Coach, you know my sixteen year old brother, Lowell?"

"Yes, Ed, I met him once."

"Well Coach, he has been in trouble with the law. He is now out on bail. While he has been waiting for sentencing, he has worked two jobs to prove to this community and to the courts that he is turning his life around. He is determined to support his sixteen year old wife and three-month-old daughter.

"Today I went to his sentencing. Other guys who had more charges against them than Lowell had, only received probation. Lowell got one to four years in Jackson prison." Ed screamed at me over the phone.

"What kind of God do we have that would allow such an injustice!"

"Ed, I have to ask you a question."

"Go ahead," he angrily shouted.

"Ed, is Lowell a child of God?"

"No," he answered.

I shouted to Ed over the phone. "Then how does he expect to get any help from God?

"You see, Ed, you are now talking with a guy who didn't get help from God for twenty-six years. Even though I thought I was a Christian, I found out later that I had never had an encounter with Jesus. Even though I prayed many times I never had prayers answered. Ed, do you think God is going to help anyone who rejects Him? All unbelievers have not accepted His Gift of eternal life, therefore they have rejected it. No way will God help them until they accept Him!

"Ed, instead of being mad at me and God, you should go down to the jail and tell your brother, Lowell, about Jesus."

Ed had now calmed down. "I can't talk to him, Coach. Would you please go down and see if he will talk to you?"

The next morning I called the sheriff, and asked if there was some time that week I could talk to Lowell. The sheriff told me that in two hours Lowell was headed for Jackson prison.

I asked the sheriff if I could drive over right then and see him. He gave permission, and I drove over to the Centreville jail where I was able to talk with Lowell in a private room.

Lowell accepted Jesus.

Then his concern turned from his prison sentence to his wife and daughter. "Coach Eby, would you please go over and tell Mindy about Jesus?"

"Lowell, I will go over and see if God opens the door."

I knocked on the door and a lady opened it. I asked for Mindy. She was sitting in the middle of the living room floor, feeding her three-month-old daughter. I introduced myself and sat down by her on the floor. I opened up God's Word and told her about Jesus. She also professed Jesus.

Lowell is now out of prison. He and Mindy are in a position to get help from God. But even as Christians, they will not receive help from God unless they follow God's spiritual program for their lives consistently. *Neither will we!*

I Can't Imagine You Being A Coach

I was the resource person at a teenage retreat. There were thirty-six teenagers, one minister, two counselors and myself. I spoke with the group at seven different sessions and spent much additional time talking with individuals.

On Saturday night we had the typical around-the-fireplace meeting. It was inside. All lights were out, just the light from the flickering fireplace. I had the group seated in chairs in a large three-quarter circle with each one facing the fireplace.

I said, "Gang, I am going to ask all of us to sit quietly and meditate with our Lord. I will ask Jack to strum softly on his guitar, and anyone who wants to can hum softly, God is good, God is good, God is good.

"Let us all see if we can get real close to our Lord. Let us see if He will flood this gathering with the Holy Spirit. Let us see what God can really do in our lives. If nothing happens, I will dismiss in prayer and we can go back to playing games and visiting."

I meditated with my Jesus that He would do something within ten minutes or I would close in prayer. At the nine-minute mark, a young lady who had refused to join the circle but who sat in the doorway of an adjoining room with her boyfriend, burst into the middle of the circle.

She had one arm up and she was crying. "I am tired of pretending, I am tired of pretending, I am tired of pretending, I need to get right with God. I need to get right with God right now!"

Two of her girl friends in the circle rushed over to her and put their arms around her and started crying with her. All three started talking to each other about Jesus. The Holy Spirit was really moving now among the group. Teenagers came to me and to the sponsors to get right with God.

As I came back to the circle after talking to a group of several teenagers who accepted Jesus, Jake rushed across the circle and grabbed my two hands. Jake was a senior in high school and was an outstanding athlete.

The sponsors had warned me about him. "Coach, you will have to keep a close eye on this Jake. He is only here to cause trouble. He doesn't believe in spiritual things." Therefore, I had especially tried to make friends with Jake.

As Jake grabbed my hands, he looked directly into my eyes and spoke. "Coach Eby, I can't imagine you being a coach. Every coach I've had has cursed me up one side and down the other. They have chewed me out, and called me vulgar names. I just can't imagine a guy like you being a coach."

I held both of his hands and looked him right in the eyes. "Jake, God has His people everywhere. But that is not the issue. Do you know Jesus?"

"I'm trying," he answered softly.

"Now is the accepted time, Jake." As I showed Jake God's wonderful plan, he accepted Him. I prayed with him as he joined the Family of God and became my brother in Christ.

After the meeting ended, I believe that half of those thirty-six teenagers had accepted Jesus, and the other half had rededicated their lives to Him.

The minister stood and before the closing prayer he spoke. "If we have a moving of the Holy Spirit in all our churches like we evidenced in the lives of these teenagers tonight, God will turn this world upside down for Jesus in a few short months."

Why Doesn't Everybody Accept Jesus?

I was speaking to a group of teenage boys and girls at a public high school, who had agreed to come to school one hour early to hear me speak. The group consisted of about thirty teenagers, several coaches, and the principal. The principal used to be one of my high school coaches.

After I closed the message, I mentioned to the principal, "Ron, if any of these students wish to talk to me separately or in small groups, could I use some office? I will write them an excuse to get into class when they leave the office." The principal agreed.

Ten came to see me. As I was talking to the last two, in walked Craig, the principal's son.

"Coach Eby, I don't know why I came in," he said. "I really don't understand why I came to talk with you. I am not really one small bit interested in spiritual things."

"Well, Craig, why don't you sit down with George and Jane. You know them, so you ought to feel at home. Besides, you can leave any time you want to. You also can turn me off any time you want to." Craig sat down and fifteen minutes later all three accepted Jesus.

Craig was amazed. "Coach Eby, is that all there is to it, in joining the Family of God?"

"According to these scriptures, Craig, that is the only way we can come into the Kingdom of God. God keeps it simple, so I and all others can understand it."

Craig wanted to say something. "Then I have a question for you, Coach. Why doesn't everyone accept Jesus?"

"That is my question also, Craig. I don't really have the

answer to that one."

Craig and a friend came to hear me speak a couple of times, and he wrote to me. The last I knew, Craig was still growing in the Lord.

I Really Don't Want To Hear It

Ned was an ex-Navy man, and an alcoholic. He couldn't keep a job because of his drinking. He spent any money he made or received for alcohol, and also much of the money his wife made. Naturally, the family, including three beautiful children, were very much in debt and struggling financially as well as in many other ways.

Ned's wife, Lila, was a Christian, but he was not in the least interested.

Lila always wanted me to come over and talk with him. I insisted that Ned invite me over himself. One day Lila told me that Ned had consented and had asked me to come over. I drove over to their house. After shaking hands with Ned, I asked him if it was alright to talk with him about the Bible and Jesus. He nodded his agreement.

I only talked about three minutes. I noticed that he was not really interested.

"Ned, you really are not interested in this, are you?"

"Not really," he answered. "I just thought it would please the wife."

"I am very sorry that I came, Ned, and I am going to leave right now. It is not right for me to force Jesus onto you. I apologize for the three minutes I talked to you, and I asked your forgiveness." I then left.

After "Calling God's Tower" was published, Ned secured a copy and read it. I received a beautiful letter from him indicating that he was now really searching for Jesus.

Some time later Ned and his wife showed up for my Wednesday night Bible Study in my home. Ned sat quietly through the entire Bible Study. Just before I was going to close in prayer, Ned asked me if he could say something.

"I would like to tell this group that two months ago, you wouldn't have caught me dead in a meeting like this. I have been an alcoholic for years. Each early morning I would start drinking and continue until late at night. I spent the money my family needed for alcohol. I have been mean and vicious. I really had nothing to live for except alcohol.

"Then I read Coach Eby's book. I started reading the Bible and praying. About one month ago I woke up in the morning, and I had lost my desire for alcohol. I had an incredible feeling come over my entire being. I felt real peace for the first time. I knew I now had something to live for. I thank God for a praying wife and children. I am not a Christian yet but I have come a long ways in thirty days."

"Brother Ned, I believe you are already a Christian. I believe the Holy Spirit entered your being and took the taste of alcohol away from you. You have something good going for you if you will just stay on His program for your life."

Brother Ned has stayed on the program. What a transformation in his life and in his family! He now has an excellent job and a beautiful relationship with his family and his God. He is also serving his Lord as president of the society for foster children. How I praised God for praying wives like Lila who never give up. Jesus didn't give up on me, either.

What Did You Come For?

I answered my phone one night at 6:30. "Coach Eby, you don't know me but I am Penny. I have problems. Would you come down to help me?"

"Penny, I have just 30 minutes before my next Bible Study. Tell me where you live and I will come down for a few minutes."

I introduced myself and sat down in a chair in her mobile home. Penny started telling me about her problems. The problems were involved around a man. Most women's problems concern men, and most men's problems concern women.

"Penny, I don't want to hear all your problems with this man."

"What did you come for?" she asked.

"I came to tell you about Jesus if you are willing to listen."

"I will listen," she agreed.

Twenty minutes later, Penny accepted Jesus and joined the Family of God. After praying with her, I said, "Penny, I am going to a Bible Study right now in my home. Wouldn't you like to come along?"

She not only went with me that night, but she has been coming ever since, including services at the church. She is now studying a disciple course to learn how to tell others about Jesus.

Since that first time I met Penny, I have never once heard her complain about anything. She just keeps praising God. As I drove past the post office the other day, Penny on the sidewalk shouted at me. "Hi Brother Eby." "Hi Sister Penny," I yelled in return. How sweet Christian fellowship is.

I Was Going To Stab My Wife

"Coach Eby, this is Delbert from Detroit. Do you remember me?"

I had met Delbert just once.

"Coach, I just came home to my wife. I am really mad at her. I threw her to the kitchen floor. I took my knife and I was going to stab her to death. Just before it happened I thought of you. I went to the phone and called you."

"Delbert, pick me up at the airport. I will be there in an hour and a half." He picked me up and took me to his house where I met his wife, Leslie, and their one-year old son.

I gave them some Bibles and went through God's plan for their lives. They accepted Jesus. I prayed with them. How quickly can God change hate into love.

Before we left for the airport, Delbert and Leslie were hugging and kissing each other, brought together through the love of Jesus! I praise God for this family as I have had sweet Christian fellowship with them for the past two years.